Death March

The Complete Software Developer's
Guide to Surviving "Mission Impossible" Projects

Death March

The Complete
Software Developer's
Guide to Surviving
"Mission Impossible" Projects

Edward Yourdon

To obtain a Prentice Hall PTR mailing list, point to:
http://www.prenhall.com/mail_lists/

Prentice Hall PTR
Upper Saddle River, New Jersey 07458
http://www.prenhall.com

Library of Congress Cataloging in Publication Data

Yourdon, Edward.
  Death march: managing "mission impossible" projects / Edward Yourdon.
    p.   cm.
  Includes bibliographical references and index.
  ISBN 0-13-014659-5 (alk. paper)
  1. Computer software--Development. I. Title (paperback edition).
QA76.76.D47Y677 1997   97-2951
005.1'068--dc21   CIP

Acquisitions editor: *Jeffrey M. Pepper*
Editorial/production supervision: *Kathleen M. Caren*
Interior design: *Gail Cocker-Bogusz*
Cover design director: *Jerry Votta*
Jacket design: *Scott G. Weiss*
Jacket Illustration: *Howard Kingsnorth/Masterfile*
Manufacturing manager: *Alexis R. Heydt*
Editorial Assistant: *Linda Ramagnano*
Marketing Manager: *Dan Rush*

© 1999, 1997 by Prentice Hall PTR
Prentice-Hall, Inc.
Upper Saddle River, New Jersey 07458

Prentice Hall books are widely used by corporations and
government agencies for training, marketing, and resale.
The publisher offers discounts on this book when ordered in bulk quantities.
For more information, contact Corporate Sales Department, Phone: 800-382-3419;
FAX: 201-236-7141; E-mail: corpsales@prenhall.com
Prentice Hall PTR, One Lake Street, Upper Saddle River, NJ 07458.

Printed in the United States of America
10 9 8 7 6 5 4 3 2 1

ISBN 0-13-014659-5

Prentice-Hall International (UK) Limited, *London*
Prentice-Hall of Australia Pty. Limited, *Sydney*
Prentice-Hall Canada Inc., *Toronto*
Prentice-Hall Hispanoamericana, S.A., *Mexico*
Prentice-Hall of India Private Limited, *New Delhi*
Prentice-Hall of Japan, Inc., *Tokyo*
Prentice-Hall (Singapore) Asia Pte. Ltd., *Singapore*
Editora Prentice-Hall do Brasil, Ltda., *Rio de Janeiro*

TABLE OF CONTENTS

PREFACE

Our achievements speak for themselves. What we have to keep track of are our failures, discouragements, and doubts. We tend to forget the past difficulties, the many false starts, and the painful groping. We see our past achievements as the end result of a clean forward thrust, and our present difficulties as signs of decline and decay.

Eric Hoffer

Reflections on the Human Condition, aph. 157 (1973)

I know . . . you're intrigued by the title of this book, and you decided to peek inside to see what it's all about. But, you're busy, busy, busy—and you don't know if you have the time to read yet another book about managing software projects. *Especially* if it's a book that tells you how things should be done in an ideal world where rational men and women make calm, sensible decisions about the budget, schedule, and resources for your software project.

However, you may have noticed that we don't live in an ideal world—and chances are that your project requires you to interact with people who seem anything but rational and whose decisions hardly seem calm or sensible. In other words, you're working on a *death march* project. The wonderful thing about the title of this book is that I don't even have to explain it. Every time I mention it to friends and colleagues, they just laugh and say, "Oh, yeah, you must be talking about *my* project!"

These days it's likely to be my project, and your project, and everyone else's project too—we're *all* working on death march projects. It seems to me that the first question you should be asking yourself (though it may not occur to you until the end of your project) is: "Why on earth did I let myself get suckered into such a project?" I'll discuss this in the first chapter, because my experience as a consultant—visiting and observing many such projects from the sidelines—is that the world would be a healthier place if more of us had the guts to stand up and say, "Hell, no! I won't join this death march!"

But, assuming there's no escape—e.g., there are no other jobs available or you've got some form of a "golden handcuff" relationship with your employer that strongly discourages you from leaving—the next question is: "How can I survive this project without ruining my health, my sanity, and my dignity?" If you're an optimist, you might even be wondering how you can conquer the obstacles before you to finish the death march project on time and under budget. But, if you've been through a number of these projects before, you probably know that the odds are stacked against you and that survival is the best you can hope for.

Having worked in the software industry for over 30 years, I find that our profession has a rather interesting reaction to death march projects. In some parts of the industry, especially in Silicon Valley, such projects are glorified as a test of fortitude, somewhat akin to climbing Mount Everest barefoot. I felt this way during my first few software projects back in the mid-1960s, and the fact that the same attitude prevails a generation later suggests to me that it's likely to be a permanent phenomenon, as long as technology continues to change as rapidly as it has been during my lifetime. Ours is not a mature industry. Every year there's a new Mount Everest to climb and a new crop of hotshot programmers who are convinced that they can run barefoot all the way to the top.

Another segment of our industry, however, regards death march projects as embarrassing failures. We've all been bombarded with statistics about the prevalence of schedule delays, budget overruns, buggy software, disgruntled users, and outright project failures. We've been told repeatedly by consultants, gurus, and methodologists that the reason for all these embarrassments is that we've been using the wrong methods (or no methods at all), or the wrong tools, or the wrong project management techniques. In other words, death march projects exist because we're stupid or incompetent.

If you talk to battle-scarred veterans in the field—the ones who have gone through a couple of death march projects and have learned that it's really not fun to climb Mount Everest barefoot—you'll often hear them say, "Hey! I'm not stupid! Of *course* I would like to use the right methods and tools and project management approaches. But, my senior management and my end users won't let me. The reason we have such a ridiculous schedule for this project is that it was imposed upon us on the first day, before we had the faintest idea what the project was all about!" Conclusion: Death march projects occur because senior managers are Machiavellian bastards and/or because our users are naive and unrealistic.

No doubt there's some truth to all this. We do make a lot of stupid mistakes managing our projects, our senior managers do indulge in ridiculous political games, and our end users do make unreasonable demands on us. I'm convinced that much of this is due to the rapid pace of change, combined with the usual disrespect that each new generation has for the advice offered by the previous generation. Why on earth should today's generation of Java-oriented hotshots pay any attention to the advice offered by my generation, whose formative programming experience took place 30 years ago in Autocoder and assembly language? And, how should today's generation of business users know what kind of Web-based application is reasonable to ask for, considering that their predecessors were asking for mainframe-based, on-line systems, with character-based, dumb-terminal interfaces?

Whatever the explanation for the phenomenon, I've come to a sobering conclusion: *Death march projects are the norm, not the exception.* I think that today's software developers and project managers *are* pretty smart and are eager to manage projects in a rational way; I also think that today's business users and senior managers are much more computer-literate than they were a generation ago and much less naive about what software developers can be expected to deliver with finite resources. That doesn't stop both groups of smart individuals from embarking upon yet another death march project—because the competitive business pressures demand it and the new technological opportunities invite it. The business managers may be fully aware that a rational schedule for their new system would require 12 calendar months, but they'll also tell you emphatically that unless it's available in six months, the competition will grab the entire market for their new product or service. And, the technical staff may be fully aware that new technologies like the Internet are still quite risky, but they will tell you that if the new technology *does* work, it will provide a strategic competitive advantage that makes it well worth the risk.

To put it another way, industry surveys from organizations such as the Standish Group, as well as statistical data from metrics gurus such as Capers Jones, Howard Rubin, Paul Strassmann, and Larry Putnam, suggest that the *average* project is likely to be 6 to 12 months behind schedule and 50 to 100 percent over budget. The situation varies depending on the size of the project and various other factors, but the grim reality is that you should *expect* that your project will operate under conditions that will almost certainly lead to some degree of death march behavior on the part of the project manager and his or her technical staff. If a project starts off with these high-risk factors, there's going to be a lot of overtime and wasted weekends, and there's likely to be a lot of emotional and physical burnout before the end of the project. Even if the project begins in a reasonably calm, rational fashion, there's a good chance that it will deteriorate into a death march project as time goes on—either because the original schedule and budget will turn out to have been highly unrealistic, or because the user will add more requirements to those upon which the original schedule and estimate was based.

So the real questions are: If you can't avoid death march projects, how can you survive them? What should you do to increase your chances of success? When should you be willing to compromise—and when should you be willing to put your job on the line and resign if you can't get your way? *That* is what this book is about. As you will come to realize, the solution will involve issues of peopleware, processes and methodologies, as well as tools and technologies. If you're going to manage a death march project, should you insist on the freedom to staff the team with people of your own choosing? Should you take a hard-line approach with process methodologies like the SEI-CMM model, or should you let the project team abandon all formal methodologies if they feel it will help them accomplish the job? Should you insist on adequate programming languages, workstations, and CASE tools—or is it more important to fight your political battles over the issues of people and processes?

These issues are as relevant to the manager in charge of the project, as they are to the technical staff that actually does the hard work of designing, coding, testing, and documenting the system; I'll address both groups in the chapters that follow. A word about managers and technical staff members: Some of the comments you'll see in the following chapters will imply that management is "evil" and that the project team members are innocent, downtrodden victims. Obviously, this is not the case for all projects and all companies, though the very existence of a death march project is usually the result of a conscious management decision. While the project team members may be willing participants in such projects, they usually don't propose them in the first place.

If you've decided at this point that you don't have time to read this book, here's a simple word of advice that may provide some value for the time you've invested in reading the preface: *triage*. If you're on a death march project, it's almost certain that you won't have the resources to provide all the functionality or "features" requested by the end user within the allotted schedule and budget. You'll have to make some cold-blooded decisions about which features to sacrifice and which ones to focus your resources on. Indeed, some of the frivolous features will *never* be implemented, and it's best to let them die on their own. Other features are important, but also relatively easy to implement, e.g., because they're by-products of the vendor-supplied class library or CASE tools that you're using. To use the medical metaphor of triage, these features will survive on their own. The difference between success and failure on a death march project often lies in the project team's ability to identify the critical features of the system that would "die" without an investment of substantial resources and energy.

Of course, there's more to surviving a death march project than just triage (I'll cover triage in Chapter 3). We also need to look at peopleware issues, "process" issues, and issues of tools and technology. I've tried to be as concise as possible, so you should be able to finish the whole book in a couple of hours; if nothing else, it should give you a more realistic assessment of your next death march project.

However, please don't get the impression that this is a "bible," or that it will provide "silver bullet" solutions to all of your problems. There are no guaranteed right answers in this book; what works in some companies and in some situations may not work in others. Equally important, the compromises that some managers and technical staff members are willing to make will prove unacceptable to others. I'll make what I consider to be reasonable suggestions, but it's up to you to decide which ones will work in your environment.

I also intend, on an ongoing basis, to collect advice from the field on my Web site at http://www.yourdon.com—from real project teams that have some practical tips on best practices, worst practices, and "breathalyzer test" questions. Even if you don't have enough money in your project budget to buy this book (such penny-pinching budgets are an indicator unto themselves of the risk associated with a death march project!), it won't cost you a penny to check the Death March Web page.

Whatever you decide to do, best of luck on your next death march project. And remember the words of Samuel Beckett:

> Ever tried. Ever failed. No matter. Try Again.
> Fail again. Fail better.

Samuel Beckett
Worstward Ho (1984)

1 chapter

INTRODUCTION

It is only possible to succeed at second-rate pursuits—like becoming a millionaire or a prime minister, winning a war, seducing beautiful women, flying through the stratosphere or landing on the moon. First-rate pursuits—involving, as they must, trying to understand what life is about and trying to convey that understanding—inevitably result in a sense of failure. A Napoleon, a Churchill, a Roosevelt can feel themselves to be successful, but never a Socrates, a Pascal, a Blake. Understanding is forever unattainable. Therein lies the inevitability of failure in embarking upon its quest, which is none the less the only one worthy of serious attention.

Malcolm Muggeridge

"Woman's Hour," radio broadcast, August 5, 1965, Quoted in *Muggeridge through the Microphone*, "Failure" (1967)

What are death march projects? Why do they happen? Why would any-one in his or her right mind agree to participate in such a project?

To many grizzled veterans, these are rhetorical questions. Every project, in their experience, is a death march project. Why do they happen? Because corporations are insane, and as consultant Richard Sargent commented to me, "Corporate insanity is doing the same thing again and again, and each time expecting different results." [1] Why do we participate in such projects? Because, as consultant Dave Kleist observed in a recent e-mail note,

> "death march projects are rarely billed as such, and it takes a lot of work when being hired from the outside to discover if your hiring company is prone to creating death march projects." [2]

If you think the answers to these questions are obvious, feel free to jump to the next chapter. I'm beginning to think they are obvious, since people rarely ask me what I mean by "death march."

1.1 DEATH MARCH DEFINED

I define a death march project as one whose "project parameters" exceed the norm by at least 50 percent. This doesn't correspond to the "military" definition, and it would be a travesty to compare even the worst software project with the Bataan death march during the Second World War, or the "trail of tears" death march imposed upon Native Americans in the late 1700s. Instead, I use the term as a metaphor, to suggest a "forced march" imposed upon relatively innocent victims, the outcome of which is usually a high casualty rate.

In most software death march projects, this usually means one or more of the following constraints has been imposed:

- The schedule has been compressed to less than half the amount of time estimated by a rational estimating process; thus, the project that would normally be expected to take 12 calendar months is now required to be delivered in six months or less. Because of the pressures of business competition in today's global marketplace, this is probably the most common form of death march project.

- The staff has been reduced to less than half the number of people that would normally be assigned to a project of this size and scope; thus, instead of a project team of ten people, the project manager has been told that only five people are available. This may have come about as a result of someone's naive belief that a new CASE tool or programming language will magically double the team's productivity—despite the fact that the team was given no training or practice with the new technology, and probably wasn't even consulted about the decision to use the technology in the first place. More commonly, though, it happens today because of downsizing, reengineering, and various other forms of staff reduction.

- The budget and associated resources have been cut in half. This is often the result of downsizing and other cost-cutting measures, but it can also be the result of competitive bidding on a fixed-price contract, where the project manager in a consulting firm is informed by the marketing department that, "the good news is we won the contract; the bad news is we had to cut your budget in half in order to beat out the competition." This kind of constraint often has an immediate impact on the number of project team personnel that can be hired, but the consequences are sometimes a little more subtle—e.g., it may lead to a decision to hire relatively inexpensive, inexperienced junior software developers, rather than higher-cost veterans. And, it can lead to a pervasive atmosphere of penny-pinching that makes it impossible for the project manager to order pizza for the project team when they spend the entire weekend in the office working overtime.

- The functionality, features, performance requirements, or other technical aspects of the project are twice what they would be under normal circumstances. Thus, the project team may have been told that they need to squeeze twice as many features into a fixed amount of RAM or disk space as their competitor. Or, they may have been told that their system must handle twice the volume of transactions that any comparable system has ever processed. Performance constraints may or may not lead to a death march project; after all, we can always take advantage of cheaper, faster hardware, and we can always search for a more clever algorithm or design approach to accomplish improved performance (though, given the constraint of a project deadline, there is a limit even to the incredible ingenuity of the human brain). But, doubling the functionality—i.e., the available features—usually means doubling the amount of work that must be carried out and that *does* lead to a death march project.

The immediate consequence of these constraints, in many organizations, is to ask the project team to work twice as hard, and/or twice as many hours per week as would be expected in a "normal" project. If the normal work week is 40 hours, a death march project team is often found working 13- to 14-hour days, six days a week. Naturally, the tension and pressure escalate in such environments, so that the death march team operates as if it is on a steady diet of Jolt cola.

Another way to characterize such projects is:

> A death march project is one for which an unbiased, objective risk assessment (which includes an assessment of technical risks, personal risks, legal risks, political risks, etc.) determines that the likelihood of failure is > 50 percent.

Of course, even a project without the schedule, staff, budget, or functionality constraints just described could have a high risk of failure, e.g., because of hostile politics between the IS/IT department and the user community. But most commonly, the reason for the high risk assessment is a combination of the constraints I've just described.

1.2 CATEGORIES OF DEATH MARCH PROJECTS

Not all death march projects are the same; not only do they involve different combinations of schedule, staff, budget, and functionality constraints, but they come in different sizes, shapes, and flavors.

In my experience, *size* is the most important characteristic that distinguishes one death march project from another. Consider four different ranges of projects:

- *Small-scale projects*—the team consists of less than ten people who are working against nearly impossible odds to finish a project in three to six months.
- *Medium-sized projects*—the team consists of 20 to 30 people, who are involved in a project expected to take one to two years.
- *Large-scale projects*—the project consists of 100 to 300 people, and the project schedule is three to five years.
- *Mind-boggling projects*—the project has an army of 1,000 to 2,000, or more (including, in many cases, consultants and subcontractors), and the project is expected to last seven to ten years.

For a variety of reasons, small-scale death march projects are the most common in the organizations that I visit around the world today; and happily, they have the greatest chance of succeeding. A tight-knit group of less than ten people is more likely to stick together through thick and thin, as long as the commitment isn't for more than six months or so; and a group of highly motivated people is more likely to be willing and able to sacrifice their personal lives (not to mention their health!) for three to six months, as long as they know that the regimen of long nights, wasted weekends, and postponed vacations will come to an end in a matter of months.

The odds of successful completion drop noticeably with medium-sized projects, and disappear almost completely with large-scale projects. With larger numbers of people involved, it's more difficult to maintain a sense of cohesive team spirit; and the statistical odds of someone quitting, being run over by a truck, or succumbing to the various perils of modern society increase rapidly. What's crucial here is not just the number of people involved, but the time-scale: working 80-hour weeks for six months may be tolerable, but doing it for two years is much more likely to cause problems. And, even though a manager might be able to convince a small group of techno-nerds to make such a sacrifice, it's almost impossible with larger project teams; statistically, the chances are much higher that some of them will be married, or will have some outside hobbies.

As for the "mind-boggling" death march projects, one would have to wonder why they exist at all. Perhaps the systems development efforts associated with the NASA project that landed a man on the moon in 1969 could be considered a successful example of a death march project; but, the vast majority of such projects are doomed from the beginning [3]. Fortunately, most senior managers have figured this out, and most large organizations (which are the only ones that could afford them in the first place!) have banned all such projects. Government organizations, alas, still embark upon them from time to time; appeals to "national security" or some other heart-warming emotion may be sufficient to blind senior management to the reality that success is virtually impossible.

In addition to project size, it may also be useful to characterize the "degree" of a death march project by such criteria as the number of user organizations that are involved. Things are hard enough when the project team only has to satisfy one user, or one group of homogeneous users within a single department. Enterprise-wide projects are usually an order of magnitude more difficult, simply because of the politics and communication problems involved in cross-functional activities of any kind. As a result, the systems development projects associated with business reengineering projects often degenerate into a death march status— even though the development effort is modest in terms of hardware and software effort, the political battles can paralyze the entire organization and cause endless frustration for the project team.

Finally, we should distinguish between projects that are incredibly difficult, and those that are fundamentally impossible. As John Boddie, author of *Crunch Mode*, points out,

> The combination of excellent technical staff, superb management, outstanding designers, and intelligent, committed customers is not enough to guarantee success for a crunch-mode project. There really are such things as impossible projects. New ones are started every day. Most impossible projects can be recognized as such early in the development cycle. There seem to be two major types: "poorly understood systems" and "very complex systems." [4]

This still leaves unanswered the questions of why a rational organization would embark upon such a project, and why a rational project manager or technical person would agree to participate in such a project. We'll deal with those questions below.

1.3 WHY DO DEATH MARCH PROJECTS HAPPEN?

If you think about what goes on in your organization, it's not difficult to understand why death march projects occur. As Scott Adams, author of the incredibly popular "Dilbert" cartoons, points out,

> When I first started hearing these stories [about irrational corporate behavior] I was puzzled, but after careful analysis I have developed a sophisticated theory to explain the existence of this bizarre workplace behavior. People are idiots.
>
> Including me. Everyone is an idiot, not just the people with low SAT scores. The only difference among us is that we're idiots about different things at different times. No matter how smart you are, you spend much of your day being an idiot [5].

Perhaps it's too depressing to imagine that you're an idiot, and that you're surrounded by (and managed by!) idiots. Or perhaps you consider it an insult that someone would even make such a suggestion. In that case, Table 1.1 shows a more detailed list of reasons for the occurrence of death march projects:

Politics, politics, politics.
Naive promises made by marketing, senior executives, naive project managers, etc.
Naive optimism of youth: "We can do it over the weekend!"
The "start-up" mentality of fledgling, entrepreneurial companies.
The "Marine Corps" mentality: *Real* programmers don't need sleep!
Intense competition caused by globalization of markets.
Intense competition caused by the appearance of new technologies.
Intense pressure caused by unexpected government regulations.
Unexpected and/or unplanned crises—e.g., your hardware/software vendor just went bankrupt, or your three best programmers just died of Bubonic Plague.

TABLE 1.1   Reasons for death march projects.

While the items in Table 1.1 may seem obvious, they're worth discussing—because they may indicate that your death march project is *so* crazy and irrational that it's not worth participating in at all. Indeed, even without an explicit rationale of the sort shown in Table 1.1, you should seriously consider whether you want to spend the next several months (or years) attached to such a project (we'll discuss that topic later in this chapter).

1.3.1 Politics, Politics, Politics

Many software developers vow that they won't get involved in politics— partly because they've learned that they're not very good at playing political games, but also because they feel that everything about politics is repugnant. Alas, it cannot be avoided; as soon as you've got two or more people involved in some joint enterprise, politics exist.

But, when politics become the dominant force in a large, complex project, you're likely to find that it degenerates into a death march. Remember my definition of a death march project: it's one where the schedule, budget, staff, or resources are 50 to 100 percent less than what they should be. *Why are these constraints being placed on the project?* There are many possible explanations, as we'll see in the discussion below; but in many cases, the answer is simply, "Politics." It may be a power struggle between two fast-track managers in your organization, or the project may have been set up to fail, as a form of revenge upon some manager who stepped on the wrong toes at the wrong time. The possibilities are endless.

The chances are slim that you'll get the appropriate politicians to admit what's going on; however, if you're a technical staff member, it's not unreasonable to ask your project manager whether the entire death march project is a political sham. Even if you don't like politics, and even if you think you're a political neophyte, listen carefully to the answer your manager gives you. You're not stupid, and you're not *that* naive. If you have a sixth sense that there's some ugly politics dominating the entire project, chances are you're right; and, if your immediate supervisor gives you a naive or ambiguous answer to your questions, you should draw your own conclusions.

What if your manager openly agrees with you? What if he or she says, "Yes, this whole project is nothing more than a bitter power struggle between Vice President Smith and Vice President Jones."? If that's the case, then why on earth is your manager participating in the project? As we'll see in Section 1.4 below, there may be many reasons; but, your manager's reasons are not necessarily *your* reasons. The existence of ugly politics doesn't mean that you should abandon the project or quit your job right away, but it does mean that you should keep your own priorities, objectives, and sense of ethics separate from what's happening on the project—for it's quite likely that many of the decisions that take place (beginning with the schedule/budget/resource decisions that defined the project as a death march in the beginning) are not being made with the best interests of the user or the enterprise in mind. If the project succeeds at all, it's likely to be an accident—or it may be because the intended victim (e.g., your project manager, or a manager several levels above your immediate manager) is a cleverer politician than the opposition counted on.

1.3.2 Naive Promises Made by Marketing,
Senior Executives, Naive Project Managers, etc.

Naiveté is often associated with inexperience, so it's not surprising to see unrealistic commitments being made by people who have no idea how much time or effort will be required to build the system they want. In the extreme case, this can lead to what my friend Tom DeMarco calls "hysterical optimism," which is when everyone in the organization desperately wants to believe that a complex project, which has never been attempted before, but which has been realistically estimated to require three calendar years of effort, can somehow be finished in nine months.

The naiveté and optimism extend to the technical staff too, as we'll see. But for the moment, let's assume that it's your manager, or your marketing department, or the end user who is responsible for the naively optimistic schedule or budget. The question is: How will they react when it eventually becomes clear that the initial commitments *were* optimistic? Will they extend the schedule, increase the budget, and calmly agree that things are tougher than they had imagined? Will they thank you for the heroic efforts you and your colleagues have made up to that point? If so, then it may turn out that the most important thing you need to do is to replace the classical waterfall life cycle with a RAD approach, so that a realistic assessment of schedule, budget, and resources can be made after the first prototype version of the system is delivered.

However, in many death march projects, this kind of rational mid-course correction isn't possible. This can happen, for example, if a senior manager makes a naive promise to the customer, and then feels that the commitment has to be honored—no matter what. In the worst case, the person making the commitment knows full well what's going on. (It's particularly apparent when the marketing manager confesses to the project manager over a beer after the celebrations accompanying a new contract from some gullible client, "Well, we wouldn't have gotten this contract if we told the client how long it would *really* take; after all, we knew that our competitors would be coming with some really aggressive proposals. And besides, you guys always pad your schedules and budgets anyway, don't you?")

The last comment is especially onerous if it comes from your boss, or from some manager two or three levels above you. It suggests that the entire process of estimating schedules and budgets is a negotiating game (which I'll discuss in detail in Chapter 3). But, there is also likely to be some degree of naiveté, for the unspoken implication in your manager's complaint about "padding" the schedule and budget is that you *could* finish the death march project in time to meet the ridiculous deadline that has been imposed upon you. On the other hand, it could have something to do with the "Marine Corps" mindset, discussed in Section 1.3.5. Similarly, the commitment to a ridiculous schedule and budget by the marketing department could turn out to be another form of politics, discussed earlier; that is, the marketing representative probably doesn't care whether or not the schedule and budget he or she proposed is ridiculous, because his or her primary objective is the sales commission, or meeting quota, or pleasing his or her boss.

Assume for the moment that the death march project has been created as a result of "pure" naiveté, absent of politics or other malicious influences. The question is: What should you do about it? As noted, a key question is the likelihood that the decision makers will revise their budgets and schedules when it becomes apparent that the original commitments can't be met. This is difficult to predict in advance, though it wouldn't hurt to check around and see what has happened to other death march projects in similar situations. (If this is the first such project that has ever occurred in your company, then you really are in uncharted territory!)

If you have the strong impression—either from your political instincts or from the experiences of previous projects in your organizations—that management will hold fast to its original budget and schedule, no matter how much of a "denial of reality" is involved, then you need to make a much more fundamental decision about whether or not to proceed. Some of this involves the extent to which you can negotiate other aspects of your project—e.g., the technical staff that will be assigned to the projects—which we'll discuss in Chapter 2.

1.3.3 Naive Optimism of Youth:
"We Can Do It over the Weekend!"

Though management is a convenient scapegoat for many of the idiotic decisions associated with death march projects, the technical staff is not entirely blameless. Indeed, in many cases, senior management will happily admit their naiveté and lack of experience with the process of estimating and scheduling complex projects. "How long do you think it will take?" they'll ask the technical hotshot, who may have been promoted to the rank of first-level supervisor just last week.

And, if the technical hotshot is ambitious and filled with youthful optimism (which often resembles the teenage delusions of immortality, omnipotence, and omniscience), the answer is likely to be, "No problem! We can probably knock it out over the weekend!" A really good software engineer—well, "hacker" might be a more appropriate description here—is firmly convinced that he or she can develop *any* system in a weekend. Minor details like documentation, error-handling, editing of user inputs, and testing are so boring that they don't count.

If you're the naively optimistic software engineer responsible for making the death march estimate, chances are that you don't even know what you're doing. You probably read the last paragraph, bristled at the apparent insult, and muttered, "Damn right! I really *can* build any system over the weekend!" God bless you; maybe you'll succeed. In any case, nothing that you hear from an old fart like me is likely to change your mind.

But, if you are a battle-scarred veteran, and you can see that you're about to be roped into a death march project because some naive young technical manager has made a ridiculously optimistic commitment regarding the project's schedule, budget, and resources, what should you do? The best advice, I think, is: "Run!" When such technical managers realize that they are in over their heads, they often collapse, resulting in truly irrational behavior or paralysis. In most cases, they haven't dealt with anything before that was so big and complex that it couldn't be overwhelmed by sheer cleverness or brute force (e.g., 48 hours of non-stop coding over the weekend). In any case, they're certainly not in the mood to hear you say, "I told you so!" as their project falls behind schedule.

1.3.4 The "Start-up" Mentality of Fledgling, Entrepreneurial Companies

I've not only watched this occur, I've participated in such projects and have been responsible for initiating them in several cases. As this book is being written, it appears that any start-up company with the name or "Java" in its corporate name or product name can get more venture capital than it knows what to do with. But in general, start-up organizations are understaffed, underfinanced, undermanaged, and outrageously optimistic about their chances of success. They have to be because a cautious, conservative manager would never dream of starting a new company without tons of careful planning and a large bank account to deal with unforeseen contingencies.

So, almost by definition, a large percentage of the projects associated with start-up companies are death march projects. A large percentage of these projects will fail; a large percentage of the companies will fail with them. C'est la vie—that's what high-tech capitalism is all about (particularly in the U.S.). Having been raised in this culture all my life, I think it's perfectly normal (my attitude is also colored by the fact that I've been lucky enough to succeed in a few such ventures). Indeed, this scenario is often one of the *positive* reasons for embarking upon a death march project, as I'll discuss in more detail in Section 1.4.

Not everyone is familiar with the culture and environment of a corporate start-up. If you've spent the past 20 years of your career working with brain-dead COBOL zombies in a moribund government agency (or, for that matter, most banks, insurance companies, or telephone companies) and you've just taken a job with a start-up firm because you were downsized, outsourced, or reengineered, then you probably have little or no idea what you're in for. Death march projects occur in big companies too, but they're often staffed by extras from *Night of the Living Dead*. The environment is completely different in start-up company death march projects; it's like a rush of pure adrenaline.

At the same time, start-up companies often suffer from the kind of naive optimism I discussed. Many start-up companies are founded by technical hotshots convinced that their new technology will make them richer than Bill Gates; others are founded by marketing wizards who are convinced they can sell Internet-enabled refrigerators to gullible Eskimos. Optimism is important in any start-up venture, and the success of the corporate venture may depend on doing what nobody has ever been able to do before. But, even an aggressive, optimistic start-up company has to obey the basic laws of physics and mathematics. If you get involved in a start-up company death march project, check to see whether there is some kind of plan for success, or whether the whole venture is based on wishful dreaming.

1.3.5 The "Marine Corps" Mentality: *Real* Programmers Don't Need Sleep!

Start-up companies are sometimes vulnerable to the "Marine Corps" syndrome, but I've seen it most often in the consulting organizations like EDS and the Big-6 accounting firms. It may reflect the personality of the corporate founder(s), and it may reflect the corporate culture in its earlier days. The corporate behavior at Microsoft, for example, has often been attributed to these factors. In essence, you'll be told by the appropriate manager, "Every project is like this, because that's how we do things around here. It works, we're successful, and we're damn proud of it. If you can't handle it, then you don't belong here."

Whether an attitude like this is civilized, humane, or right is a topic for separate discussion. Indeed, whether it's even successful is another question. The important thing is to realize that it's *deliberate*, not accidental. If you're a martyr or a revolutionary, you might decide to attack the corporate culture. But, chances are that you won't succeed. It's quite possible that there will be some negative long-term consequences of the overall death march culture, e.g., the best people may slowly drift away, and the company may eventually fail. But, when it comes to *this* death march project, there's no point questioning why it has been set up with a nearly-impossible schedule and budget. Like the prototypical manager of such a company says, "If you can't handle it, then you don't belong here."

Sometimes there's an official rationale for such corporate behavior—e.g., "We compete in a tough marketplace, and all of our competitors are just as smart as we are. The only way we succeed is to work twice as hard." And sometimes, death march projects are set up to weed out the younger (weaker) junior employees, so that only the survivors of the death march projects will reach the exalted status of "partner" or "Vice President." Whatever the rationale, it's usually fairly consistent; there's not much point complaining about it for the sake of a single project.

That doesn't necessarily mean that you should accept an assignment on such a project; after all, just because every other project within the organization is a death march doesn't necessarily mean that yours will succeed or that you will survive. It simply means that the decision to create such a project has an understandable origin.

1.3.6 Intense Competition Caused by Globalization of Markets

Organizations that might not have tolerated death march projects in the past are sometimes being forced to do so in the 1990s, simply because of the increased level of competition associated with the global marketplace. The secondary factors here are universal telecommunications (including the Internet) and governmental decisions to open previously protected markets or eliminate tariffs and quotas.

For some organizations, this is not a new phenomenon. The automobile and electronics industries, for example, have been facing stiff competition since the 1970s. But, for other organizations, the appearance of European or Asian competitors in the North American marketplace can come as a rude shock. Once senior management has accepted the reality of serious competition, it may decide to embark upon a variety of radical moves, ranging from downsizing to reengineering; but, it may also decide to compete head-on with a new product or service that requires a new, ambitious system to support it. Voila! A death march project has begun.

Such projects are often accompanied by dire predictions from senior management of the consequences of failure—e.g., layoffs, or even corporate bankruptcy. And, as I'll discuss below, this may prove to be the primary justification for participating in such projects.

1.3.7 Intense Competition Caused by the Appearance of New Technologies

Competition from an expanded marketplace is often perceived as a defensive issue, but it can also be perceived as an aggressive, proactive opportunity—"If we build this new system, with double-byte characters, then we can offer our company's products for sale in Japan." Similarly, the introduction of radically improved technology may cause a defensive response from a company that was reasonably happy with products built around an older technology; or, it may lead to a proactive decision to utilize the new technology for competitive advantage. At the time this book was being written, technologies like Java and the World Wide Web were an obvious example of this phenomenon; but, the amazing thing about our industry is that new examples appear every few years.

If the corporate response to the new-technology situation is essentially defensive in nature, then the death march project may be one that seeks to exploit the company's *old* technology far beyond its normal limits. Thus, if the organization has too much invested in the old technology (and the infrastructure surrounding it) to abandon it entirely, it may embark upon a rewrite of its old systems, with demands that the programmers find ways to make it ten times faster and sexier.

Many death march projects in this category are the ones that involve first-time usage of new technologies. Think back to the first client-server, object-oriented, relational database, or Internet/Java projects in your organization; some of them may have been modest experiments to explore the potential benefits of the technology, but some of them were probably created as a competitive response to another company's introduction of the same technology. And in the latter case, these projects can be huge, as well as being saddled with outrageously aggressive schedules and budgets.

But what really contributes to the death march nature of such projects—beyond the obvious characteristics of size, schedule, and budget—is the attempt to use bleeding-edge technology for an industrial-strength application. Even if the technology is basically usable, it often does not scale up well for large-scale usage; and, nobody knows how to exploit its strengths and avoid its weaknesses; and, the vendors don't know how to support it properly; and on, and on . . .

While all of this may be perceived as an unpleasant experience by the older technical project team members (the ones who remember the "good old days" of FORTRAN II and assembly language), it's important to remember that the younger technicians and project managers *prefer* these new technologies, precisely because they *are* new. And these are the same folks that I characterized above as naively optimistic about the schedule and budget constraints within which they're working. Is it any wonder that projects degenerate into a death march, with everyone working late nights and long weekends to coax an experimental new technology into some semblance of working order?

1.3.8 Intense Pressure Caused by Unexpected Government Regulations

As mentioned above, one of the reasons for death march projects associated with globalization of markets is the decision by governmental authorities to reduce tariffs, eliminate import quotas, or make other such decisions to "open" a previously closed market. But this is just one example of governmental influences that can lead to a death march project. Deregulation of controlled industries or privatization of government agencies are two other obvious examples. Indeed, many of the death march projects taking place today around the world are a direct result of a government decision to deregulate the telecommunications industry, the financial services industry, the airline industry, and so on.

However, there are also many instances of *increased* regulatory pressure from governmental authorities—especially in the areas of taxation, reporting of financial details to stock-market authorities, environmental regulations, and the like. In any kind of democratic society, there's likely to be a great deal of advance notice about such regulations, because the legislative body argues and debates and fusses over details for months or years before the relevant legislation is enacted. But, often the details aren't clear until the last moment, and the typical reaction from senior management is to ignore the whole thing until it becomes an unavoidable reality. And thus, another death march project is created.

The particularly onerous thing about many of these government-mandated death march projects is the deadline: The new system *must* be operational by some arbitrary date, like the first of January, or fines of a million dollars a day will be imposed. There may be an opportunity to ask for an extension or a waiver, but in many cases, the deadline is absolute. And the consequences are usually as dire for the organization as those mentioned above: layoffs, bankruptcy, or other calamities will occur if the new system isn't finished on time.

Notice that in projects like these, technology is usually not the issue; what characterizes projects as being death march in nature is the aggressive timetable. Of course, management sometimes complicates the situation by understaffing the project, or hobbling it with an inadequate budget.

1.3.9 Unexpected and/or unplanned crises

Your two best programmers have just marched into your office to inform you that (a) they're getting married, (b) they're joining the Peace Corps, and (c) today is their last day on the job. Or, your network services manager calls you to say that your vendor has just gone bankrupt and you'll have to reprogram everything in the next 30 days to use another vendor's network protocol. Or, your legal department calls you to say that the company has been sued for ten zillion dollars because the company is not in compliance with Sub-paragraph 13(b) of Regulation Q of some arcane tax code that nobody even knew about. Or, . . .

Of course, you could argue that in a well-managed company, the impending departure of your two best programmers would have been anticipated and planned for. And you wouldn't have been so silly as to be wholly dependent on one telecommunications vendor. And management would have had the foresight to check into the details of Regulation Q. Such crises, according to the purist, are the result of poor planning and poor management; an "unplanned crisis" is therefore an oxymoron.

Perhaps so; but as a practical matter, it's becoming more and more difficult to anticipate and plan for all the crazy things that can happen in the business world. For better or worse, we live in a world of chaos, and death march projects are a natural consequence of this chaos. Indeed, even if we have a general idea that chaotic things *could* occur in the future, we may still have to respond to them in a death march fashion. Everyone in the vicinity of the San Andreas fault in California, for example, knows that a truly massive earthquake will occur sooner or later; but, that won't prevent a rash of death march projects from starting up the day after the "big one" drops the western half of the state into the Pacific Ocean.

Indeed, even when we know *precisely* when a crisis will occur, it often leads to a death march project—because management's tendency is to avoid dealing with the situation until the last possible moment. How else can we explain the panic that is creeping into many IS/IT organizations as the Year 2000 problem looms ahead of us? We've known for a *long* time that January 1, 2000, was coming, and we've known that it was a deadline that could not be postponed. We've known precisely what the nature of the problem is, and it doesn't require new-fangled technologies like Java. So, why is it that I'm so certain that death march Year 2000 project teams are forming while I write this book in the summer of 1996, and that even more frantic projects will be initiated in 1997, 1998, and 1999?

In any case, unforeseen crises can lead to all kinds of death march projects. In the worst case, they create projects for which the deadline is "yesterday, if not sooner"—because the crisis has already occurred, and things will continue to get worse until a new system is installed to cope with the problem. In other cases, such as the unplanned departure of key project personnel, it can turn an otherwise rational project into a death march exercise because of the resulting shortage of manpower and the loss of key intellectual resources.

For various reasons, these often turn out to be the worst kind of death march projects *because nobody anticipated that it would turn out this way*. For the "Marine Corps" situation discussed above, there are no surprises. Everyone knows from the first day of the project that this one, like all previous projects, is going to require extraordinary effort. And, for the start-up companies, the death march project is anticipated with excitement; not only will it be exciting and challenging, but its success could make everyone rich.

1.4 WHY DO PEOPLE PARTICIPATE IN DEATH MARCH PROJECTS?

The theme of the discussion in the previous section is that organizations create and/or tolerate death march projects for a number of reasons. We may agree or disagree with those reasons, and we may sympathize with the ones caused by truly unexpected crises—but ultimately, as individuals, we must accept them as a fact of life.

But, that doesn't mean we must participate in them. Most of this book presumes that you *will* participate in a death march project, though I will specifically suggest that you resign under certain circumstances. But the best time to do so, in most cases, is at the beginning. When told that you have been assigned to such a project (either as a manager or a technical staff member), you should consider saying, "No, thanks! I'll pass on this one." If that's not an acceptable response within your corporate culture, you almost always have the option of saying, "No, thanks! I quit!"

Obviously, some developers—and probably a larger number of managers—will argue that this is not a practical choice for them. I'll discuss this detail shortly, but for now, it's sufficient to note that it's one of several possible "negative" reasons for participating in a death march project; it may not be fun, but perhaps it's not as bad as the alternatives.

On the other hand, some developers (and some managers) *gladly* sign up for such projects; aside from the issue of naive optimism, why would any rational person volunteer to participate in a project that's likely to require 14-hour days, 7-day weeks, and a year or two of postponed vacations?

The most common reasons are summarized in Table 1.2; I'll discuss them below.

The risks are high, but so are the rewards.
The "Mt. Everest" syndrome.
The "buzz" of working intensely with other committed people.
The naiveté and optimism of youth.
The alternative is unemployment.
It's required to be considered for future advancement.
The alternative is bankruptcy or some other calamity.
It's an opportunity to escape the "normal" bureaucracy.
Revenge.

TABLE 1.2 Reasons for participating in death march projects.

This is not meant to be a complete list. Kevin Huigens [6] asked his project team to do a little brainstorming at one of their recent staff meetings, and they came up with the following list of explanations for participation in death march projects:

Everybody wants to feel wanted.

Perceived opportunity.

Perceived money gain.

Can't afford to lose job.

Brought in from the outside to lead the project.

Willing suspension of disbelief.

Don't care whether project fails, get to work with cool technology.

On-the-job-training on new technology.

Eternal optimism.

Challenge.

Plain stupidity.

Chance to prove yourself.

To get the job done.

It's the only project.

Your friend is running the project.

Your brother is running the project (it'd take more than friendship).

Your boss said so.

You have no other life.

Nothing better to do.

Stock options.

Existing pay vs. expectation of raise.

Love is blind.

Resume building.

Ignorance.

Camaraderie.

Expectations for how long it will take are too low.

Of course, all of this assumes that you know in advance that it *is* a death march project. As consultant Dave Kleist [7] observed, that's not always so easy when you're interviewing for a new job:

> ... it's rarely printed as part of the want ad. Not much sense in saying, "Are you interested in working incredible hours for no additional benefit beyond your hiring salary?" ... Seriously, death march projects are rarely billed as such, and it takes a lot of work when being hired from the outside to discover if your hiring company is prone to creating death march projects.

And, as Steve Benting [8] pointed out, sometimes you get taken by surprise:

> ... it seems to be a well-thought-out project this time. You've got someone leading who has a real sponsor in management, the project plan appears to be solid, the people involved all appear to be good. Hell, you *want* to work on this thing. Then it collapses because your sponsor gets taken out in a political struggle, the project plan turns out to be built on assumptions that are incorrect, and one or two key people turn out to be flaky. You can learn to watch out for them, but sometimes you misjudge. And you don't want to believe that it's happening again.

1.4.1 The Risks Are High, But So Are the Rewards

The start-up company scenario discussed in Section 1.3.4 is a good example of this situation. If you tell a project team that the success of their project will mean the company can go public, and that their stock options will make them instant millionaires, they'll happily work until they drop. They realize—at least in an intellectual way—that there are risks associated with the venture; but, since many of them still believe that they're immortal and omnipotent, they don't pay much attention to the risks.

Indeed, considering the influences of Western culture (especially in the U.S.), it's not at all surprising to see young software developers voluntarily sign up for death march projects. We've been told in countless ways that the success of movie stars, rock singers, sports heroes, and Olympic athletes, as well as business executives and software entrepreneurs, depends largely on tireless energy, enormous commitment, long hours, and personal sacrifice. We never hear about the guile and duplicity, the shady deals, and illegal activities that are sometimes associated with success. And, we rarely hear anything about luck and the importance of being in the right place at the right time. Bill Gates, for example, certainly exhibits all the textbook characteristics of a successful business executive; but, if a group of IBM executives hadn't shown up in Seattle in 1980 to look for a PC operating system, and if Gates hadn't been available when IBM was unable to meet with its originally intended OS contractor . . . well, who knows where Microsoft would be today?

And one more thing: We don't hear enough about the real consequences of the "sacrifices" that a death march project usually requires—sacrifices, that is, in the areas of personal health, mental health, and personal relationships. None of these are likely to matter very much to a 22-year-old technical person, and they often don't matter to the introverted, antisocial people who are attracted to the computer field. On the other hand, it's small wonder that you'll find fewer people in their mid-40s and 50s volunteering for death march projects; not only have they learned that most of these projects really *are* doomed to fail, but they've also learned (usually the hard way!) that it's not worth sacrificing their marriages and good relationships with their children.

Ultimately, this is a personal choice, based on personal values. I'm in no position to tell anyone else what's right or wrong. I should emphasize, though, that I'm not as negative as one might think from the comments above. Though I believe that I'm much less naive than I was 30 years ago, I'm still attracted by entrepreneurial opportunities. Show me a sufficiently exciting risk/reward formula, and I'll sign up for yet another death march.

Incidentally, sometimes the rewards are psychological rather than financial. As Sharon Marsh Roberts [9] observed:

The "heros" are needed, wanted, desired. They are certain of their place in history, if only they can keep this project from outright sinking under its own weight.

The same people take on EMT work and enjoy fire-fighting (literally). If you only win once in ten times, but everybody else lost all ten, wouldn't you be a hero, too?

Paul Neuhardt [10] put it another way:

For me, it was ego, pure and simple. They told me that they just *knew* I could help prevent the project from becoming a death march. I was made the "technical project manager," given ego boosts on a regular basis, then hung out to dry along with the rest of the team. Left, right, left, right, left, *plop!*

1.4.2 The "Mt. Everest" Syndrome

Why do people climb dangerous peaks like Mt. Everest, despite the pain and risk? Because it's there. Why do people run a marathon and drive themselves to the point of physical collapse in triathlons? Because of the challenge. It's all the more exciting if the challenge is one that has never yet been successfully accomplished; of the five billion people on the planet, for example, only one can stand before us and say, "I was the first to walk on the moon." Some may think it's crazy, egotistical, and selfish to even try, but others are willing to brave the odds and deal with horrendous obstacles for the private thrill and public glory of succeeding. As consultant Al Christians [11] remarked to me in a recent e-mail note,

I am somehow prompted to reply "testosterone," which is about the same as "because it's there." There are plenty of jobs that raise the "why?" question. Underground mining, cowboying, logging, smoke jumping, jet fighting, submarining, even high rise window washing all have serious drawbacks far beyond what you describe for software projects, and yet all these have practitioners whose sense of self is linked to their profession.

And so it is with death march software projects. I had the chance to visit the original Macintosh project in the fall of 1983, a few months before the product was officially unveiled, and I was humbled by the intensity of the team members' commitment to their challenge. In addition to whatever other reasons they might have had for working long hours and dealing with Steve Jobs's megalomaniacal ego, the team members were utterly convinced (partly as a result of Jobs's charisma) that the Macintosh would revolutionize personal computing. They were lucky—they turned out to be right.

From this perspective, even death march projects that fail can be *noble* failures. Countless projects in Silicon Valley have fallen into this category, often after burning tens of millions of dollars of venture capital; the pen-based computing projects of the early 1990s are just one example. But, even though they failed so badly that entire companies went bankrupt, and though they caused divorces, ulcers, and nervous breakdowns—even though they did all of this and more—the people who worked on those projects still speak of their experiences in hushed tones. "I worked on the operating system at Go! Corp.," a grizzled veteran will tell her awestruck apprentice. "Now *that* was a revolutionary piece of software!"

Though it may never reach the front pages of *Computerworld*, there are also numerous death march projects with lofty ambitions buried within large organizations—with application developers signing up gladly because the "corporate Mt. Everest" seems such a worthy challenge. Sometimes these projects fail because the marketplace, or the corporate end users, don't want and don't need the glorious, revolutionary systems being developed; sometimes they fail because the project team bit off more than it could chew and promised more than it could deliver.

There are two things to watch for if you find yourself being swept up in the hysteria of a Mt. Everest-style death march project. First, watch out for the projects that are predetermined failures. Suppose, for example, that someone told you that you could be on the first mission to Mars, and that you would even have the honor of being the first person to plant a foot on Martian soil. "Of course," your project manager would go on to say, "you won't have any oxygen tanks, because we won't have enough room on the space craft for all that extra weight. So it's a guaranteed fact that you're going to die—but think of the honor and the glory!" [12] I'll discuss these projects in more detail in Chapter 3 (under the heading of "Kamikaze" projects), but for now, the scenario speaks for itself.

The second thing to watch out for is that the challenge being described by your corporate management (or by the entrepreneurial founder of your software company) may not turn out to be such a big deal after all. This is a particularly insidious danger if the challenge is technical in nature, e.g., "We'll be the first people on earth to put an operating system with the functionality of Windows 95 into 4K of ROM!" Granted, that would be an amazing technical accomplishment—but so what?

It's a good idea to ask the "So what?" question two or three times—i.e., *continue* asking the question in response to each successive answer you get from your corporate management. If the response to the Windows 95 scenario posed above is, "Well, that means we could put *all* of Windows 95 onto your wristwatch!" then ask, "So what!" again. In some cases, the answers will eventually become silly, and you'll be jerked back into the real world. For example, suppose your boss answers the second "So what?" question above with the explanation, "Well, if we can also squeeze in a full voice-recognition system, that means you'll be able to write Visual Basic programs while you're walking down the street, by talking to your wristwatch!"

No doubt there are a few dozen programmers who would say, "Cool!" and volunteer to spend the next three years of their lives on such a project. The fact that nobody in his right mind would ever use such a project is irrelevant to them; the technical challenge is sufficient justification. Putting Windows 95, full voice recognition, and Visual Basic into 4K of ROM would give you supreme bragging rights at any convention of hackers and programmers; if that's what you live for, then by all means, go ahead and sign up for the project.

It's also a good idea to explain the project in simplified non-technical terms to your spouse, or your "significant other," or your parents—or, even better, your children. *They* will ask the "So what?" question, without the burden of being tempted by the technical challenge. "You're going to give up your nights and your weekends and your vacations for the next two years in order to put Windows 95 on a wristwatch?" your spouse will ask incredulously. And your children will ask, "Yeah, but Mom/Dad, why would anyone *do* that?" If you can answer those questions without feeling utterly foolish, then you can sign up for the project with a clear conscience.

A worse form of the Mt. Everest project is the one where the challenge matters *enormously* to corporate management, but not at all to anyone who stops and thinks about the situation for a second. "Why are we signing up for this death march project, boss?" the young programmer asks innocently. "Because," the boss thunders righteously, "it will increase our corporate earnings per share by a full 3.14159 cents!" This means that if the programmer is lucky enough to have options on a hundred shares of the company's stock, and if every penny of increased earnings is paid out in dividends, the programmer would get a whopping $3.14; and, if Wall Street gets so excited by all of this that it boosts the price of the stock by a dollar, the programmer's net worth would increase by another hundred dollars. "And what else would I have to show for the thousands of hours of overtime you're asking me to sign up for, boss?" the young programmer asks. The boss is silent, for he knows that the honest answer is: *nothing*. The project is intrinsically boring, involves no interesting technology, and has a 75 percent chance of failing anyway.

But, the very worst death march projects, in my opinion, are the ones where the boss deliberately manipulates the innocent project team into believing that a Mt. Everest-style challenge is involved, when the boss knows full well that it's not. Imagine the project team member who asks, "Why are we trying to build this batch, mainframe, COBOL airline reservation system in six months, boss?" The boss is likely to respond, "Because *nobody* in the entire airline industry has ever tried to do it in less than three years before!" I suppose that one could argue that there *is* a technical challenge involved in creating a batch-mode airline reservation system, but it's not the kind of technology that I would want on my resume in the late 1990s. In any case, what makes this scenario a death march project is not the technical challenge, but the ridiculous schedule imposed on the project. Why is the project manager doing it? Who knows—but it's not likely to be the sort of thing you'll want to brag about to your friends a year from now.

1.4.3 The Naiveté and Optimism of Youth

Ours is a young industry, and many of the most exciting and challenging projects are being performed by, and led by, people in their 20s. It's not at all uncommon to see death march projects where the entire technical team is under the age of 25. As such, they remind me of the fighter pilots and bombing crews recruited by the Air Force in the Second World War and Vietnam War: young, idealistic, and absolutely convinced that they could do *anything*. As David Maxwell [13] put it:

> Projects are like a marriage. We tend to start off naively and full of hopes and slowly as reality sets in, we have to reassess our expectancies within the relationship. There are many reasons apart from *logic* that attract people together into a marriage and it is the same case with projects. With a predominantly youthful work-force, it is likely that the "death march" project will occur again and again as a training ground for managers and developers alike. And, as I know from personal experience, I often repeat the same mistake many times before the penny drops.

Indeed, it's this supreme confidence that enables a death march team to succeed where traditional project teams have failed. Part of the folklore of our industry is that the most successful products—ranging from Lotus 1-2-3 to Netscape Navigator—have been developed by a handful of people under conditions that no "rational" project team would have accepted. When these projects succeed, they often bring fortune and fame to the project team; and when they fail, they often provide some valuable lessons to everyone involved (though the corporate consequences may still be disastrous!).

It's important to note that the naiveté and optimism of youth are usually combined with enormous energy, single-minded focus, and freedom from such distractions as family relationships. Obviously, youth doesn't have a monopoly on any of this, but it's a lot more common to see a 22-year-old programmer willing and able to focus on the technical demands of a death march project for 100+ hours per week, continuously for a year or two, than a 35-year-old programmer with a spouse and two children and a moderate passion for mountain climbing. The young programmer who signs up for a death march—as well as the relatively young project manager who optimistically promises success to the corporate chieftains—is implicitly saying, "Of *course* I'll succeed with this project; I'll overwhelm the obstacles with sheer energy!"

I won't make any value judgments about all of this, because it's pointless. As noted above, ours is an industry that attracts young people, and I don't think that will change in the next few years. I also don't think it's unlikely that young people will abandon their optimism, energy, and ability to focus single-mindedly on a problem. As for their naiveté . . . well, it doesn't help much for battle-scarred veterans to accuse their younger colleagues of this disease.

1.4.4 The Alternative Is Unemployment

Because we *do* have an industry populated by young, optimistic people, and because it's a vibrant industry that has been growing steadily (and sometimes rapidly!) for the past 30 to 40 years, I'm always surprised to hear this explanation for participation on death march projects.

But, we're also in an industry where rapid change renders some veterans obsolete. Indeed, there has been such enormous change during this decade that our profession—like so many other white-collar professions—has experienced significant downsizing, reengineering, and outsourcing. Aggregate employment in the software industry may be rising steadily, but we sometimes forget that this means only that C++ programming jobs are increasing more rapidly than COBOL jobs are declining [14]. Additionally, the large IS/IT shops that have expanded into bureaucracies of several thousand people have been particularly vulnerable to reengineering and downsizing; senior management may not be ready to reduce the ranks of technical staff, but they're often eliminating the middle managers, administrators, and staff people.

All of this figures significantly in death march projects. Perhaps the reason your project team has only half as many people as it should is that management has cut the entire software organization in half. And the reason that your project schedule is twice as demanding as it should be is that management is attempting to reengineer by edict: The entire organization must be twice as productive as before, which translates into the simple commands of, "Work harder! Work faster!" [15]

This is not a book about reengineering, and I don't want to comment on the reengineering strategies employed by management. The significant issue here is that many technical staffers and project managers feel an implied threat when projects are created in this kind of environment. Oftentimes, if they don't agree to the death march project parameters, they'll be the ones to lose their jobs. For the 22-year-old, unmarried programmer, this shouldn't be a problem; for the 35-year-old project supervisor with a family and a mortgage, it can be a more serious problem. And, for the 45-year-old programmer whose only skills are COBOL and CICS, it can be a serious problem indeed. Even though we do have a young industry, it's been around long enough that there are even some 55- and 60-year-old programmers who are grimly holding on until their pension is fully vested.

It's also common for middle-aged or older people to find that they're locked into a community, because their spouse has a job in the same town, or their children can't be pulled out of the local schools, or because the prospect of leaving behind aging parents and other family members is too painful. None of this seems a problem when the job market is growing, but anyone living in Poughkeepsie, New York today knows exactly what I'm talking about. People living in Redmond, Washington could conceivably find themselves faced with the same kind of rude shock 5, 10, or 20 years from now.

I'm generally sympathetic to the middle-aged and older software professionals who find themselves in this position, though the reengineering/downsizing phenomenon has been around long enough that I'm amazed to find technical people who ignore the possibility that it could happen to them. But this, too, is a subject for a different book; I've discussed it at length in my books *Decline and Fall of the American Programmer* and *Rise and Resurrection of the American Programmer*, and I'll confine my remarks here to the *reality* of such death march projects.

If your company has told you—either explicitly or by innuendo—that your job will disappear unless you sign up for a project with a ridiculous schedule, budget, and resource allocation, what should you do? Obviously, this depends on your assessment of your financial, physical, emotional, and psychological situation; but, you also need to assess the situation within your company accurately. In some cases, the real threat is that your promotion, bonus, or salary increase will be withheld if you don't participate (I'll cover this separately below). But, even if the threat is termination of employment, big companies can't usually carry out their threat right away; you may have two or three months before your job disappears, and that may be enough time to find a job elsewhere.

What if the threat is more immediate and blunt? "Sign up for this death march project right now, or pack up your things and get out!" says your boss. It's inconceivable to me that a rational person would choose to work in such an environment, but let's assume the environment had been reasonably friendly until the latest reengineering craze turned your boss into a raving lunatic. So, here you are: sign up, quit, or be fired. What can you do?

If at all possible, my advice is to quit now, because it's only going to get worse. You may have to live off your savings for a few months, and you may even have to take a pay cut while you gain experience in some newer technology, but chances are you'll be a happier person than if you knuckle under and continue on in a situation that has little or no upside potential. Sometimes you can accomplish this by volunteering for the death march project while simultaneously updating your resume and starting the job search, though this can create some ethical dilemmas if you feel that quitting in the middle of the death march project would leave your teammates stranded and helpless.

If you feel that you are truly stuck—because of imminent pension vesting, or because of unmarketable technical skills, or because personal commitments keep you locked into a one-employer town—then you might be tempted to take a more positive approach to the death march project. "By gosh, I'll show them that there's still some bark left in this old dog," the middle-aged veteran will say. "I'll show management that I'm still just as good as those young whippersnappers, and we'll get this project done on time!" The courage and positive outlook are admirable indeed, but just remember one thing: If your death march project succeeds, there will be another one. Remember the theme at the beginning of this book: *Death march projects are not the exception, they have become the norm.*

1.4.5 It's Required to be Considered for Future Advancement

As described, there are times when the "invitation" to join a death march project carries with it a threat that future promotions and raises will be contingent upon (a) acceptance, and (b) success in the project. This is often associated with a reengineering initiative—e.g., "The people who lead the Megalith Bank into the twenty-first century will be the ones who lead us through this incredibly complex and challenging Total System 2000 reengineering project!" If you find yourself in this situation, remember that politics are a key factor. The people who eventually take credit for the success of the death march project may or may not be the people who participated in it. And the manager who proposes the death march project may be using the reengineering "crisis" solely as an opportunity to advance his or her career, with little or no concern for whether the project team members survive in the process.

If you've memorized every word of Machiavelli's *The Prince*, and if you enjoy playing political games, then such death march projects might sound like great fun. But most software professionals haven't read *The Prince* since their college days (if ever), and in addition to admitting their political naiveté, they'll also express disgust at the whole concept of politics, and enormous disrespect for those who indulge in it. If that's the case, why would anyone sign up for the Megalith Bank's Total System 2000 project? The only plausible answer: because you sincerely believe that it's a one-time death march project, and because you really believe that it will help advance your long-term career within the Megalith Bank. And if you believe this, chances are pretty good that you also believe pigs can fly.

In the majority of cases I've observed, the threat of withholding promotions and raises is part of the "Marine Corps" culture discussed earlier. Whether it's right or wrong doesn't matter at this point; what counts is that it's fairly consistent. If you receive such threats on your first death march project, you'll probably get them on your second, third, and fourth. You may have been too innocent to contemplate the long-term implications of such a policy when you first joined the company, but sooner or later it will sink in. There are really only two options in this case: accept it or quit.

1.4.6 The Alternative Is Bankruptcy or Some Other Calamity

As I explained, some death march projects have been caused by the re-engineering, downsizing, and outsourcing decisions made by senior management, which in turn were often caused by global competition, unexpected government regulations, and the like. Whatever the cause, the results are the same: The employee signs up for the project because he or she sincerely believes that the alternative is bankruptcy or some other dire calamity. And the situation is often exacerbated by provocative statements from management that anyone unwilling to participate in the death march should resign forthwith, so that those who remain can concentrate on saving the company.

Again, the issue here is not whether the situation is right or wrong, or whether management should have taken earlier steps to avoid the crisis. The point is that once the crisis has arrived and management has initiated the death march project, you need to make a rational decision about whether or not to participate. As this book is being written, Apple Computer is a good example of a company filled with death march projects as it fights for survival (though I have no personal knowledge of any managerial ultimatums to "sign up or leave").

From earlier discussions, you can anticipate my advice here: Step back and ask yourself whether this death march project is a one-time exception, or the beginning of an ongoing pattern. Even if you win the battle, your company may have lost the war; indeed, your success with your death march project may have the ironic consequence of delaying the final demise of the company just long enough to sustain a *second* death march project.

Again, this is a personal decision, and it may be colored by feelings of loyalty, sympathy, or a Hollywood-inspired desire to "win one for the Gipper"—a last hurrah to show the world that you and your company are not going to give up without a fight. And who knows: maybe a tremendous success with your death march project will turn things around, as was apparently the case when Borland delivered its Delphi product to the marketplace in early 1995. None of us has a crystal ball when it comes to predicting the outcome of a death march project, nor can we accurately predict what the consequences of a death march success or failure will really be. Some companies die quickly, others die a long, lingering death, and still others are acquired before the terminal rot sets in.

As you consult your own crystal ball, seek advice from as many people as possible—especially from those who have no vested interest in the outcome. You may find some honest, objective managers in your company who will candidly discuss the consequences of the death march failure/success; but, you should also remember that the same managers have their own careers and paychecks to worry about, and that their egos and political instincts may prevent them from sharing the really vital information you need to make an informed decision.

1.4.7 It's an Opportunity to Escape the "Normal" Bureaucracy

Technical staffers and project managers often complain that their corporate bureaucracy stifles productivity and introduces unnecessary delays into the software development process. But, the larger the organization, the more entrenched the bureaucracy—especially in organizations where the methodology police enforce strict adherence to SEI-CMM or ISO-9000 processes. Similarly, the human resources department may have elaborate procedures that must be followed before new people can be hired, or before external contractors can be used on a project.

Death march projects often provide the opportunity to circumvent some, if not all, of the bureaucracy—and this is reason enough for frustrated software developers to sign up for such projects. In the extreme case, the effort takes on the characteristics of a "skunk works" project: The project team moves out of the corporate facility into a separate building, where they can carry out their work without the distractions of the normal bureaucracy. But even in a less extreme situation, a death march project can often get permission to use its own tools and programming languages, to try new technologies like object-oriented programming, and to short-circuit much of the ponderous procedures and documentation that would otherwise be required. Equally important, the death march project manager is often given far greater latitude when selecting team members than would normally be the case.

In the best case, all of these changes can transform a death march into a civilized experience—that is, the very procedures (and technology and people) that threatened to turn the project into a death march have been removed or replaced. And, if the death march project is eminently successful, it can serve as a catalyst to make permanent changes to the technology, peopleware, and processes used in other development projects throughout the organization. Conversely, if the death march project fails, it might serve as an affirmation that the "standard" policies aren't that bad after all.

In any case, a situation like this is a perfectly plausible reason for working on a project that might otherwise seem uncivilized. In some organizations, certain software developers make a point of *always* signing up for such projects, because it's the only way to avoid getting sucked into the bureaucracy.

1.4.8 Revenge

Revenge may not seem like a rational explanation for working on a death march project, but it's real nonetheless. The success of the death march project might be sufficient to wrest power away from an incompetent Vice President, or it might serve to humiliate an obnoxious critic who continually tells you "it can't be done" within the schedule and budget constraints of the death march project. Revenge is a powerful emotion, and it is particularly evident in the senior management ranks of large organizations, where insults are remembered forever, and where crafty politicians will sometimes wait months or years to wreak revenge upon their enemies.

Revenge can be a very powerful personal motivator, but it's usually somewhat more difficult to imbue an entire project team with the emotion. And when it happens, it often creates a situation where the team loses track of the "official" objective of delivering a working system within a specified budget and schedule—after all, their first and highest priority is revenge.

If revenge is *your* motivation, then there's not much for me to say—this is another personal judgment call. But, if you're signing up for a project in which it's the manager's revenge, or the team's revenge, fueling the project (and causing it to accept deadline and budget constraints they normally wouldn't accept), then you should be very careful indeed. "The Vice President is an idiot," your project manager might tell you, "and if we finish this project in six months, he'll be so humiliated in front of the Board of Directors that he'll have to resign!" Well, that's fine—maybe the VP really is an idiot. But, do you really want to sacrifice your personal life for the next two years to bring about his or her demise? After all, the next VP is likely to be just as much an idiot as the last one.

On the other hand, if everyone perceives the Vice President to be the personification of Darth Vader, and if the project manager is seen to be a combination of Luke Skywalker and Yoda, then a death march project can be very invigorating indeed. If this is the case, the entire project is recast into a battle of Good versus Evil, and that's enough to make people accept incredible sacrifices without complaint.

1.5 SUMMARY

If the discussion in this chapter seems pessimistic and cynical, remember—it hasn't stopped death march projects from taking place. Companies both large and small are filled with politics, and staffed by managers and technical developers who suffer from mind-boggling optimism, as well as from the usual gamut of emotions like fear, insecurity, arrogance, and cruelty. And, the combination of reengineering, downsizing, outsourcing, and global competition—along with the opportunities provided by new technologies like object-orientation, client-server, and the Internet—suggests to me that death march projects are likely to be a common occurrence for years to come.

And that's the primary point of this chapter. You may not agree with any of the rationales suggested here; you may not like any of the reasons for initiating such projects or joining such projects—but they're real nonetheless. The key point is to recognize and understand your own motivations at the beginning of a death march project, so that you can make a rational decision to join the team or look elsewhere for your next job. Since many of these projects are initiated during periods of great corporate stress and emotion, rational decisions are not as easy to make as you might think; it's all too easy to be swept away by the emotions of your fellow colleagues or your manager.

By the way, this doesn't mean that I'm opposed to death march projects; I agree with my colleague Rick Zahniser [16] that such projects can be an educational experience, even if they fail:

> I've told you before, I think everyone should be on at least one of these projects. However, there are some other things that you should do at least once:
>
> • Spend a night in jail
>
> • Get commode-hugging drunk
>
> • Raise a boy
>
> • Raise a girl
>
> • Start your own business
>
> • Climb Mount Fuji

For the remainder of this book, I'm going to assume that you *have* made a rational decision to join a death march project—though I'll remind you from time to time that you always have the option of quitting during the project. We'll assume that your primary objective at this point is to succeed, or at least survive the project, and in subsequent chapters, we'll see how that can be done.

Notes

1. Ed,

A colleague of mine passed along this paraphrased quote. I think it applies here.

The definition of (corporate) insanity is doing the same thing again and again, and each time expecting different results.

I have no idea who originally framed the assertion, but it's gold!

Richard Sargent

5x5 Computing Solutions Inc.

2. Ed,

>> 1. Why would anyone in his right mind agree to work on a "death march" project (defined in the terms above)? <<

Because it's rarely printed as part of the want ad. Not much sense in saying, "Are you interested in working incredible hours for no additional benefit beyond your hiring salary? Does the idea of working endlessly on obsolete technology while 'waiting' for a slot to open up on that exciting GUI/DSS/warehouse/HTML subproject really entice you? Do you define three-tier architecture as an opportunity to hear what other project members will work on without your help?"

Seriously, death march projects are rarely billed as such, and it takes a lot of work when being hired from the outside to discover if your hiring company is prone to creating death march projects. In addition, death march projects only look that way. While they demand the hours, every hour is not productive. After a while, people find ways to do the things they are being deprived of (pay bills, run errands). It just isn't billed that way. The environment still sucks, people hate it.

And, how accurate are those hours that are being billed? Where do they come from? Got any contractors? Ever heard of "nuisance hours" or "annoyance hours"? You know, where a contractor overbills because they can't stand some of the people they are working for. (Let me say right now that I've never done it and never will do it, but know people who have). The lead or manager does what the contractor thinks is stupid, and the contractor takes revenge (in their own quiet way). And, what about overhead? Are all hours to be marked to the project, including corporate and department meetings, training, etc.?

>> 2. If a colleague of yours was about to take on the task of managing a death march project, what is the ONE THING you would advise him/her to do? <<

Try to craft an exquisite exit clause in the contract <VBG>.

Seriously, one of the reasons for a runaway is the inability of someone to hear reality, usually upper management (either side, IT or business). Someone taking over a death march has got to find an angle for them to get some maneuvering room (functionality, cost, time) in at least one aspect or they are doomed.

>> 3. Conversely: what is the ONE THING you would advise your colleague NOT to do, under any circumstances, when embarking upon such a project? <<

Acknowledge that it is going to be a death march. Doesn't sound honest but admitting that it's going to be a killer can be demoralizing for two reasons: one, people don't like to hear that the next 6-12 months could be hell; two, management usually underestimates the negatives. Not much hope if you know right out of the gate that it's going to be ugly. I had friends who worked on one project that had management openly admitting that there was going to be road-kill on the project. Oddly enough, they had trouble recruiting internal replacements once the turnover kicked in.

Seriously, admitting up front that it's out of control is already saying very little for one's management skills. If you ask, sometimes staff will volunteer ways to help keep it from becoming a death march. In the death marches I've seen, the one thing that I've seen common to them all is a lack of empowerment among the staff.

- Dave

3. Of course, the project might not have been planned as a mind-boggling project, and the prospect of ultimate doom might not have been apparent to anyone. A participant in the ill-fated Taligent joint venture between Apple and IBM reminded me of this possibility. That project, he reminded me, had previously existed within Apple under the code-name of "Pink." And, before that, it was known as SNARC (for "Sexy New Architecture"). The amazing thing, my correspondent told me, was that at any point during its seven-year lifetime, during any of its three incarnations, it was always perceived as a two-year project. That perception was true on the first day of the project, and it was a perception firmly believed by most of the managers who were still working frantically seven years later, when the project was shut down.

4. John Boddie, *Crunch Mode* (Englewood Cliffs, NJ: Yourdon Press/Prentice Hall, 1987), page 20.

5. Scott Adams, *The Dilbert Principle* (New York: HarperBusiness, 1996), page 2.

6. Ed:

At our weekly staff meeting, my team and I had a brainstorming session on your 3 questions. Here's our answers:
1. Why would anyone in his right mind agree to work on a "death march" project (defined in the terms above)?

Everybody wants to feel wanted   Perceived opportunity
Perceived money gain   Can't afford to lose job
Brought in from the outside to lead the project
Willing suspension of disbelief
Don't care whether project fails, get to work with cool technology
On-the-job-training on new technology
Eternal optimism   Challenge
Plain stupidity   Chance to prove yourself
To get the job done   It's the only project
Your friend is running the project
Your brother is running the project
  (It'd take more than friendship)
Your boss said so   You have no other life
Nothing better to do   Stock options
Existing pay vs. expectation of raiseLove is blind
Resume building   Ignorance
Camaraderie
Expectations for how long it will take are too low
2. If a colleague of yours was about to take on the task of managing a death march project, what is the ONE THING you would advise him/her to do?

Leave me out   Run!
Keep your eyes open   Ask "What's the pay?"
Get a lot of rest before you start the project
Make sure you can trust all of your co-workers
Realize the developers aren't your enemy, the managers are
Try to get management to understand the ramifications of the project
Communicate. Communicate. Communicate.
Keep the team small   Hire new graduates
Keep the team intact   Manage scope
Review the design
Focus is a substitute for time
Make sure testing plan is ready when it's time to test
Make sure you have a test plan. Make sure everybody knows what to do
Documentation is critical   Don't rush to code
Keep documentation updated and current
Everyone should have access to documentation
Have regular weekly progress meetings

Have daily progress meetings
All code works before you leave at the end of the day
Keep plenty of good coffee on hand Make sure team is happy
Make sure team has everything they need
Use management by walking around
Make sure everyone understands what they're doing
3. Conversely: what is the ONE THING you would advise your
colleague NOT to do, under any circumstances, when embarking upon
such a project?
Don't plan a wedding
Don't have unclear areas of responsibility
Don't allow design changes lightly
Don't assume 1st version is final
Don't become irritated or angry   Don't lose your cool
Don't let others lose their cool
Don't forget to back stuff up
Don't expect everyone on the team to be dedicated
Don't get too personally involved in success or failure of the
project
Don't rely too heavily on 1 member of the team
Don't allocate resources lightly
Don't assume team members understand the entire project
Don't overcommit   Don't underestimate
Don't refrain from asking questions when you don't understand
Don't start the project
Don't start the project if you haven't got the money to finish
Don't commit to unreasonable dates
Don't be afraid to quit if you feel management is unreasonable
Don't be too hard on overworked, underpaid workers
Don't let meetings last > 1.5 hours
Don't be afraid to bend the rules
Don't forget to have a life   Don't sweat the small stuff
Don't be afraid to let management know you need something
Don't be afraid to stand up to management
Don't forget to keep your resume updated
Don't accept as gospel info from so-called experts
Don't forget that management doesn't understand how to develop
software
Don't forget that shortcuts just defer work, they don't eliminate
it
Is that enough for you?
—Kevin

7. See Note #2.

8. Ed,

As long as you're asking...

>>1. Why would anyone in his right mind agree to work on a "death march" project (defined in the terms above)?<<

Because it seems to be a well-thought-out project this time. You've got someone leading who has a real sponsor in management, the project plan appears to be solid, the people involved all appear to be good. Hell, you *want* to work on this thing. Then it collapses because your sponsor gets taken out in a political struggle, the project plan turns out to be built on assumptions that are incorrect, and one or two key people turn out to be flaky. You can learn to watch out for them, but sometimes you misjudge. And you don't want to believe that it's happening again. (I'm assuming some things here. I've only been involved on one large project, but it certainly went down hard. Delivery date was October, '94 and later moved to March '95. I was working on the contingency plan towards the end and left after most of the team in January '95. The new system still does not exist. The company is now in the process of purchasing someone else's system that doesn't have half of the functionality they originally required.)

>>2. If a colleague of yours was about to take on the task of managing a death march project, what is the ONE THING you would advise him/her to do?<<

I would say to take care of his/her people as much as possible. Kick them all out of the office on Friday nights and try to make sure they're getting sleep. (Those months of 12-hour days six days per week can just burn out the developers, making them either quit or make too many mistakes.) No matter how badly the work needs to be done, you've got to take care of your people. Sometimes getting the most out of them requires sending them home. (If you know the project's in trouble when you start, you've got a long haul ahead during which you'll need good people.)

Also, make sure that you've got the best salary scale possible. It won't make all the difference, but it should be cheaper than attrition if it's enough to keep some people on.

>>3. Conversely: what is the ONE THING you would advise your colleague NOT to do, under any circumstances, when embarking upon such a project?<<

Don't let anyone put serious pressure on the employees besides you. Run interference to keep the developers free from others who are trying to ask them to run that 2-minute mile. (We had a developer working for us when I was the IS Manager -- and before the aforementioned project was started -- who was writing a new commissions system. The Sales VP came down to tell her that until she completed this system, her -- the sales manager's -- salespeople couldn't pay their mortgages. My VP quite rightly threw her out to let the developer work in peace.) That's not to say that you can't push those employees yourself, but you have to have some control over the stress levels in the organization if you're going to keep them going.

>> I'd like to solicit input, feedback, war stories, case studies, good jokes, etc.<<

This must be where I tell you about how, on that infamous project, the new President explained to me why he wouldn't sign off on requirements when asked to. (Needless to say, scope creep was a major factor in its death.) He was a down-home type who thrived on people taking his southern drawl as a sign that they were dealing with a country bumpkin. He had also just orchestrated the removal of our sponsor -- the previous President -- by killing the project. His reason for the management group's refusal to sign off on requirements was that my VP was "going to hold our feet to the fire" with that document. In other words, he wouldn't agree to sign the document because he would have to live with it later! At this time, I knew I really needed to get out of there, and quickly...

Steve

9. Ed--

>> 1. Why would anyone in his right mind agree to work on a "death march" project (defined in the terms above)? It's understandable that an inexperienced software developer (or someone who hasn't had the pleasure of reading Scott Adams' "The Dilbert Principle") might be bamboozled by management's claim that the death march is an anomaly, and that the superhuman efforts are going to revolutionize the human race, defeat Communism, cure cancer, etc. But after you've heard this pitch two or three times, it sounds like a broken record. So why do we get sucked into this again and again?<<

The "heros" are needed, wanted, desired. They are certain of their place in history, if only they can keep this project from outright sinking under its own weight.

The same people take on EMT work and enjoy firefighting (literally). If you only win once in ten times, but everybody else lost all ten, wouldn't you be a hero, too?

>>2. If a colleague of yours was about to take on the task of managing a death march project, what is the ONE THING you would advise him/her to do? (The "one thing" motif was suggested by Jack Palance in the wonderful movie "City Slicker", starring Billy

Crystal)<<
I'd encourage him to keep his sense of humor. It may be gallows
humor, but it's all that such a group has. <sigh>
>>3. Conversely: what is the ONE THING you would advise your
colleague NOT to do, under any circumstances, when embarking upon
such a project? <<
I would encourage him (and excuse me, it would be a him in 99/100
attempts) to not invest in options or get a large mortgage. You
can only take high risk in one arena at a time, without risking a
total wipeout of personal assets.
I once said that I would be willing to take a certain job whose
incumbent tended over a seven year period to last no longer than
a year. I figured that three months' salary would provide enough
savings to recover from the inevitable.
—Sharon

10. Ed,
<< 1. Why would anyone in his right mind agree to work on a "death
march" project (defined in the terms above)? >>
For me, it was ego, pure and simple. They told me that they just
KNEW I could help prevent the project from becoming a death march.
I was made the "technical project manager," given ego boosts on a
regular basis, then hung out to dry along with the rest of the
team. Left, right, left, right, left, PLOP!
(The really embarrassing thing is, I let these same people do it
to me AGAIN just one year later. Once I began to feel myself falling
into the step of the death march, I ran like hell for the door.
Me, and about 60% of the rest of the staff. BTW, It's been four
years now since I first got suckered in, and neither system has
ever seen the light of day, nor will they.)
<< 2. If a colleague of yours was about to take on the task of
managing a death-march project, what is the ONE THING you would
advise him/her to do? >>
To quote those mad Englishmen in "Monty Python and The Holy Grail"
I would say "RUN AWAAAAAYYYYYY!!!". It sounds like a flip answer,
but it isn't really. Some of the most damaging effects of a death
march project are psychological. Lower self esteem, depression,
anxiety and sudden mood swings are all behaviors I have witnessed
(and sometimes experienced) during these projects. I've seen at
least one marriage break up in no small part because the partner
involved in a death march let it consume her so totally that she
became an entirely different person, one whom her husband (and most
of the rest of us) had no desire to be around. I know another woman
who, when a three year "death march" ended with the project being

cancelled, said that it was the only experience in her life that
even approached the heartbreak she felt when she miscarried during
the sixth month of pregnancy. Now that's trauma. If you can get
out, go.

<< 3. Conversely: what is the ONE THING you would advise your
colleague NOT to do, under any circumstances, when embarking upon
such a project? >>

If you can't beat 'em, this is one case where you do NOT want to
join 'em. Do not let yourself become too emotionally attached to
the outcome of this project. Like POWs on death marches, think about
anything else but the march in order to survive. Try to go to work,
grind out your day's brick for the wall, and go home. If you want
stimulation and personal reward, read a book, join a social club,
volunteer at the local animal shelter or buy a kiln and throw some
clay pots. Do anything to keep your mind off of work as much as
possible. The moment you get too attached to the project, the guards
with the rifles win and you, the lowly POW, lose.

Paul

11.Ed

Sounds like you are going to have a lot of fun this summer.

>>1. Why would anyone in his right mind agree to work on a "death
march" project?

Since you mentioned "City Slickers", the movie that used such
regrettable sexual stereotypes, I am somehow prompted to reply
"testosterone", which is about the same as "because it's there."
There are plenty of jobs that raise the 'why?' question. Underground
mining, cowboying, logging, smoke jumping, jet fighting,
submarining, even high rise window washing all have serious
drawbacks far beyond what you describe for software projects, and
yet all these have practitioners whose sense of self is linked to
their profession.

But if you really think that reasons are needed, here are a few:

a. We think we learned so much in the last experience that it would
be a waste to not find a project on which it could be applied.

b. We know that some of our colleagues are going to be suffering,
and we don't mind doing our part to lessen their burden.

c. It's like a lottery ticket -- despite the odds, we can imagine
the possibility of large rewards if we win big.

d. The high level of urgency that arises during these difficult
projects redistributes power to those who know how to resolve
the crises, i.e. us, and we like power.

> 2. If a colleague of yours was about to take on the task of
managing a death march project, what is the ONE THING you would

```
advise him/her to do?
Remember that the people who love him/her love him/her for reasons
that have nothing to do with the project.
> 3. Conversely: what is the ONE THING you would advise your
colleague NOT to do, under any circumstances, when embarking upon
such a project?
Since "this is the way it's been for a long time, and this is the
way it's gonna continue to be," don't try to work at a pace that
you can't sustain healthfully for a long time.
Al
```

12. As I was finishing the writing of this book in late 1996, an article appeared in the *New York Times* describing a slightly modified strategy for the first mission to Mars: send the astronauts with enough food and water to live a "normal" life of 40 years on Mars, but without any fuel for their return. The rationale was that a lifetime supply of food and water would weigh considerably less than the fuel required to make a return trip. The amazing thing is that it was presented at a recent scientific conference as a serious proposal, and that approximately one-third of the conference attendees indicated that they would be willing to sign up for the one-way trip!

13. Ed,

```
As I talked on another thread the other day, projects are like a
marriage. We tend to start off naively and full of hopes and slowly
as reality sets in, we have to reassess our expectancies within
the relationship. There are many reasons apart from *logic* that
attract people together into a marriage and it is the same case
with projects. With a predominantly youthful workforce, it is
likely that the "death march" project will occur again and again
as a training ground for managers and developers alike. And, as I
know from personal experience, I often repeat the same mistake many
times before the penny drops.
Nietzsche, the German philosopher in the last century said that
"society is governed by mediocrity". What he was presumably
implying here is the central, conservative-stream will tend to
dominate behaviour and control events. This central-stream is
hell-bent on preservation from the extremes and will draw the
blinds on anything that threatens their positions. What we are
really asking for in IT is a radical re-shaping of the way projects
are managed, with open vertical and horizontal communication.. and
an openness to radicalism. This is very threatening for the central
core of the typical task, role, club organisational culture. An
Organisation with a cuture of existentialism has a much better
chance of developing good project on a regular basis but these
```

```
Organisations are still a rarity.
An old girl-friend of mine who is in a leading position in one of
the Major Business Schools regularly seeks advice from me as to
how to overcome the deluge of internal politics and methods that
are stifling their practices, certainly a case of not practicing
what they preach! In addition, Computer Science departments the
world over are paying scant regard to People and Management issues
as the Lecturers themselves are, in general, inept outside of the
technological framework.
So perhaps it is inevitable that, with an inappropriate education
and cultural backdrop, we can expect "death march" projects to
continue to be the norm... But looking at it from another
perspective, these "death march" projects are the essential grist-
for-the-mill for the few success stories that make the whole show
worthwhile.
--David
```

14. My colleagues have reminded me that in the late 1990s, COBOL programmers are actually in short supply because of the massive Year-2000 conversion projects underway. However, I believe this is a relatively short-term phenomenon; the prospects for COBOL programmers are pretty bleak after New Year's Eve, 1999.

15. This scenario is *far* more common in North America than it is in Western Europe or in the Pacific Rim countries that I've visited. While companies around the world have engaged in reengineering projects, it's less common, outside North America, to see the "radical" reengineering projects that eliminate large numbers of employees. And for the same reasons—cultural traditions, social policies, government regulations—there are fewer death march projects in these countries. The workers, especially in Western Europe, are far more likely to be shielded from excessive overtime and to refuse adamantly to give up their sick days, vacation days, holidays, personal days, and other forms of time off. Whether this is a good thing or a bad thing is outside the scope of this book.

16. Ed,

```
>>why do they do it??<<
I think they do it because, as Al, suggests, they think they're
better than others who have tried. And, sometimes they really are!
(That doesn't eliminate the death march. In fact, it probably
prolongs it.)
I've told you before, I think everyone should be on at least one
of these projects. However, there are some other things that you
should do at least once:
+ Spend a night in jail.
```

+ Get commode-hugging drunk
+ Raise a boy
+ Raise a girl
+ Start your own business
+ Climb Mount Fuji
(The Japanese have a saying:
"He who fails to climb Fuji-san is a fool. He who climbs Fuji-san
twice is an even greater fool.")
One thing to do:
Get a good manager, who is empowered to do the right things.
One thing not to do:
Kill yourself when the project goes south.
—Sr. ric

2

chapter

POLITICS

Beware the politically obsessed. They are often bright and interesting, but they have something missing in their natures; there is a hole, an empty place, and they use politics to fill it up. It leaves them somehow misshapen.

Peggy Noonan

What I Saw at the Revolution, "Another Epilogue" (1990)

The political arena leaves one no alternative, one must either be a dunce or a rogue.

Emma Goldman

Anarchism and Other Essays, "Anarchism: What It Really Stands For" (1910)

To "know your place" is a good idea in politics. That is not to say "stay in your place" or "hang on to your place," because ambition or boredom may dictate upward or downward mobility, but a sense of place—a feel for one's own position in the control room—is useful in gauging what you should try to do.

William Safire, *Before The Fall,* Prologue

Politics are a factor in *every* software development project, no matter how much we might want to deny it; the distinguishing characteristics of death march projects is that the politics are usually so intense they can overwhelm the effort to get any work done. Thus, while the *process* associated with politics, namely the political process of negotiation, will be discussed in a separate chapter, it's important to acknowledge the existence of politics in this chapter and to offer some general advice.

Many software developers will argue that while politics exist, they would prefer to steer clear of the whole ugly mess. That's understandable—many of us who gravitate to the software field are socially inept and politically naive: not only do we find political games nauseating, but we know that we won't do well if we try to play the "game" of politics. That's fine, as long as *someone* (typically the project manager) can handle the politics. But, if everyone participates in a death march project on the assumption that, "because this project is so important, they'll leave us alone and spare us the usual messy political negotiations," then the project has far fewer chances of success.

I'll discuss three aspects of politics in this chapter:

- Identifying the political "players" involved in the project
- Determining the basic nature of the project
- Identifying the levels of commitment of project participants

2.1 IDENTIFYING THE POLITICAL "PLAYERS" INVOLVED IN THE PROJECT

The key point to remember here is that your chances of success in a death march project are effectively zero unless everyone on the project team knows who the key players are. Some of them will be noisier than others, and some will be supporters and friends; but, some will be vocal opponents of the project, and others will be waiting for the chance to stab the project manager in the back. It's easy to forget this while juggling a thousand other management crises and technical problems, but it's essential.

I believe that it's imperative for *everyone* on the project to know who the key players are—even if it's the project manager's job to interact with all the external players on a day-to-day basis. On rare occasions, a "skunk works" project will manage to isolate all of the project team members from the rest of the human race while the work is being done, but that's unusual. Indeed, in today's world, even a "skunk works" project isn't completely isolated—because everyone is connected to everyone else via e-mail and the Internet. And in normal working environments, everyone is bound to have some interaction with other technical colleagues, as well as managers above and outside the project, and various members of the user community, during the course of the project. It's inevitable—we bump into them in the hallway, in the cafeteria, or in the restroom.

Thus, if a project team member receives an apparently innocent phone call, e-mail message, or casual question in the hallway from an apparently friendly middle-level manager asking, "So, how's the project coming along?" it's important for that team member to know whether the message is from a friend or foe, and whether it's thus likely to have political overtones. Whatever answer you provide to the casual question is likely to be carried back to other parts of the organization, and it's not uncommon to see the information amplified, distorted, or buried. As Dale Emery observed in an e-mail message to me [1]:

> In general, I've observed that if there is a constituency whose input is relevant, the developers will often get it anyway, though perhaps in a more expensive, more distorted way than if the manager weren't trying to keep it from them. Other times, the developers will simply make assumptions about what each stakeholder needs.

The typical "players" in a death march project are the following:

- Owner
- Customer
- Shareholder
- Stakeholder
- Champion

I'll discuss each of these below.

2.1.1 Owner

The *owner* is traditionally the person who accepts, authorizes, or pays for the system and/or the results of the project. It's obviously important to identify this person and do anything possible to keep him or her happy during the course of a death march project.

It's amazing how many software projects take place without anyone having the faintest idea of who the owner is; this is particularly common in organizations where projects are spawned by ambitious and over-eager IS/IT professionals who reassure one another with statements like, "I'll bet the marketing department will be really ecstatic when they see this new system we're building for them." Obviously, well-managed organizations would never let such projects get started—but the major point to keep in mind here is that you won't see many death march projects initiated without a clear command from an owner. The reason is simple: such projects involve extraordinary expense and/or risk and/or schedule constraints. The IS/IT department is unlikely to invent such projects on its own initiative, and the normal bureaucracy in the organization would prevent the project from being scheduled and funded unless a strong, vocal command is issued by someone willing to take authority.

This raises another interesting point: The owner of a death march project often turns out to be a much higher-level manager than would be the case for a normal software project. Indeed, it sometimes turns out to be the President or CEO of the organization, because the project affects the very survival of the company. Even if it's only a Vice President, the point is that the owner of a death march project often has much more clout, and much more latitude when it comes to authorizing expenditures and exceptions to bureaucratic restrictions, than might be the case for a normal project.

On the other hand, this doesn't mean that the rest of the political hierarchy has disappeared; indeed, one of the problems with many death march projects is that the project manager has little or no direct contact with the owner. Authorization for the project, as well as periodic demands for status reports, may be filtered down the chain of command from the high-level owner to the middle-level manager who sits just above the death march project manager. And all of these intermediate managers between the *real* owner and the project manager may be, in the terminology discussed below, either customers, shareholders, stakeholders, or champions—or political enemies of the project.

The reason it's important to keep this in mind is that the owner's original demand for a death march project can be easily distorted before the project manager receives his or her marching orders. Most often, the non-negotiable aspect of the death march project is the deadline: The new Super-Widget System absolutely, positively *must* be finished by the first of January or the world will come to an end! But, as that order is transmitted down the chain of command, the organizational bureaucracy will tack on its own list of additional constraints: The project must be programmed in a combination of Ada and RPG; the team must include George, Harriet, and Melvin (because they're so incompetent that no other project will take them); it must use the organization's newly-created (but never-before-used) object-oriented methodology; it must suffer weekly visits from the methodology police; the project team members must fill out the 17-page form XJ13 in triplicate at the end of each workday; and, . . . the list goes on.

In situations like this, a face-to-face meeting with the high-level project owner can sometimes result in all of these idiotic constraints being eliminated, by executive fiat—all except one: the deadline. But, if the project manager has a written authorization that exempts him or her from the other ridiculous rules (which may well be the reason no other project has even been finished on time!), it may be possible to finish the death march project within its required schedule constraint. And, if the high-level owner can be convinced that some extra money is needed in the budget for equipment, tools, or even a slush fund for weekly pizzas for the project team, the project manager can usually obtain it, even if the bean-counters and penny-pinchers elsewhere in the organization would normally do their best to prevent it.

Obviously, not all high-level owners are so cooperative, and not all project owners occupy lofty positions within the organization. But the point remains: While it's important for *any* project to identify its owner, it's doubly important for death march projects. And my experience has been that in a majority of cases, the high-level project owner is far more likely to be a friend than a foe. It's in the owner's interest to cut through the red tape and eliminate the bureaucratic constraints, which is almost always a blessing for the project manager.

However, keep in mind that the project owner may not be the person who actually uses the system when it's installed; nor is the owner the only one who has a political impact upon the project. The other players, discussed below, also must be kept in mind.

2.1.2 Customers

The *customer* is the person—or, in many cases, the *group* of persons— who will use the system when it is finished by the death march project team. It's common, in organizations around the world, to refer to this person (or group) as the "user." Customers may also be owners of death march projects; but, a far more common scenario is the one where the customers are administrative or clerical users who will interact with, and operate, the system developed by the death march project team.

The politics associated with project customers are discussed in most project management textbooks, and I won't cover the subject in much detail; suffice it to say that all of the politics are magnified in a death march project. We know, for example, that the customer is usually the source of the detailed requirements for a system, because the owner (and various other high-level managers) have little or no experience with the actual operation of the business application, and tend to view the operational terrain from a height of 30,000 feet. But, despite the necessity of communicating directly with the customer/users to elicit the detailed requirements of the system, we know that in many projects, the owner (or other managers) will tell the project team *not* to talk to the users because "they're too busy," or because "I can tell you everything you need to know about their requirements," or various other excuses. Finally, we know that in normal projects, the customers can ultimately sabotage the project by refusing to use it, or by complaining that it doesn't meet their needs.

All of this is true for death march projects as well, with one additional caveat: The customer(s) may not be aware of the extraordinary politics, constraints, or pressures associated with the death march project. This can create a disaster if someone on the project team marches up to a customer and says, "Hi—I'd really appreciate it if you could interrupt your work now to describe your requirements, because if our project is late, the entire company will go bankrupt. But of course, if the project *does* succeed, you'll be out of a job too, because the whole point of our new system is to facilitate a massive downsizing effort that will eliminate the entire 700-person clerical department you belong to."

2.1.3 Shareholders

Shareholders are effectively "co-owners" of a system; while they may not have the authority to initiate a project, or to accept its results, or to approve the budget, they have a vested interest in its outcome. Indeed, they *do* share the budget in many cases, along with all of the other benefits and risks associated with the project. Think of them as members of a "Board of Directors" with the owner as "Chairman of the Board." The shareholders may or may not get together on a regular basis, and they may not have any explicit contact with the project team; but they're shareholders nonetheless.

Thus, to a large extent, the project team and project manager can treat the shareholders in much the same way they treat the owner—the key point here is that the shareholders must not be forgotten or ignored. It's hard to overlook them, for they tend to throw their weight around and make their voices heard; they're also present in many of the meetings and presentations associated with the death march project. On the other hand, there's a tendency on the part of some project managers to avoid these individuals if possible, on the theory that the project owner can speak for the group—and understandably, the project manager feels that every moment spent coddling a shareholder is a moment that could have been spent working on the project. But, just as the shareholders can participate in the decision to authorize, approve, and pay for the death march project, they can be involved in the decision to cancel the project. If they feel they are being ignored, they are that much more likely to do so.

Consultant Dave Kleist identified an interesting form of shareholder in a recent e-mail communication [2]:

> In several of the death march projects I've experi-
> enced, I believe that there is a variation of shareholder
> that is very important to identify: the vendor, espe-
> cially if they have people on site to work on the
> project.

Actually, if a vendor(s) is involved, there may be several categories of shareholders. The vendor's market representative is often more concerned about making the sale and earning a commission than whether the vendor's products actually work and the project succeeds. If the vendor has installed consultants, technicians, or other individuals who will work with the project team, then a slightly different set of political agendas will emerge.

2.1.4 Stakeholders

The distinction between shareholder and stakeholder may seem academic, but it's an important one. Stakeholders are those who have a "stake" in the outcome of the project, even if they don't have an explicit decision-making role in its conduct or progress. Customers, in the sense discussed above, are obviously stakeholders, and so is the owner and other shareholders.

Other stakeholders might be members of the management hierarchy who will have to abandon their old information systems if the new system is finished on time. Or, they might be members of unions, or suppliers, customers, or competitors. They might even be other members of the IS/IT organization; for if the death march project succeeds, it could have an impact on methods, tools, or other aspects of the way "normal" projects are conducted. Paul Neuhardt pointed out another common form of stakeholder in a recent e-mail message to me [3]:

> You missed "the inner circle." These are the people
> who have no direct stake in something yet they have
> influence with those who do, an opinion on what
> should be done and a burning need to inflict their
> opinion on others. Also known as "the closest advi-
> sors," these people often spend time whispering in the
> ears of decision makers in soft, subliminal tones and

can turn a friend into a foe overnight without you even knowing that it happened.

This sounds like stakeholders are "enemies" of the death march project, and I don't mean to imply this; stakeholders can be allies and valuable supporters too. They can put in a good word during the kibitzing that inevitably takes place behind the backs of the project team members; and they can supply all kinds of assistance—tangible and intangible—to the project team if they feel it's worthy of support. Indeed, if the death march project is regarded as an "underdog" that somehow got involved in a "David vs. Goliath" battle, even those members of the organization who have no stake at all in the outcome of the project will sometimes step forward and offer support.

Notwithstanding the possibility of this kind of support, there is probably a higher likelihood that the stakeholders will be critics and enemies of the project. The reason is simple: A death march project is more likely than a normal project to represent a severe change in the status quo; and one of the basic principles of politics is that individuals and organizational cultures automatically resist a change in the status quo, even if they can be convinced intellectually that the change is important and necessary. So, while the project team obviously wants to welcome stakeholders who turn out to be friends of the project, it also needs to be alert to the possibility of stakeholders who will throw road-blocks into the schedule and the project plan.

One other point to keep in mind: The existence and identity of the stakeholders is not always obvious, because they're not part of the formal organization chart. If the system has an explicit impact on the labor union, or on the clerks in the order-entry department, then it isn't hard to identify them as stakeholders. But, if there's a crusty old project manager who plays golf with the VP of Information Systems, and if that project manager is muttering to himself, "If that death march project succeeds, then we'll *all* have to learn Smalltalk, and I'm still convinced Smalltalk is a Communist plot," then you've got a silent stakeholder that could have a subtle, but important, impact on the project.

2.1.5 Champions

Just as there are potential enemies of the death march project, there are also friends—including friends so powerful and so helpful that they come to be known as *champions*. The best of all worlds is the champion who is also the project owner; champions may also come from the ranks of customers, shareholders, or stakeholders. Champions, however, are often outside the normal set of political players in the project. The champion might be rooting for the success of a young project manager that he or she considers a protégé; or, the champion might be concerned about the overall success of the project because of the impact on the reputation and credibility of the IS/IT department or entire organization. Most often, the champion is intrigued by the technology "silver bullet" with which the death march project manager hopes to accomplish miracles—whether it's Java, OO technology, or a new client-server development tool, the champion may have seen earlier demonstrations of it, and may even have been the one who suggested that the project manager use it for the death march project.

Every project can use a champion or two, but death march projects *really* need them. The reason should be obvious from the discussion above: Projects like this already have plenty of critics and enemies, along with those who will second-guess every decision that the project manager makes. There will be numerous occasions throughout the project when someone in a management meeting will complain that, "Those hotshot techno-nerds on the Titanic Project have ordered seven copies of Visual Basic Enterprise without going through proper channels. Not only that, the project manager took $32.98 out of petty cash to buy McDonald's hamburgers and French fries for the project team last Friday. Why, I could smell the French fries all way down the hall in *my* office! [4] We can't let them get away with this blatant disregard for company policy!" The champion is the one who can stop all of this nonsense by saying, "Trust me; these kids might be a little feisty, but they'll get the job done. Leave them alone."

This won't work, of course, unless the champion has a great deal of credibility within the organization's political circles—without this, he or she is not a champion at all. But, it often means that the champion will be a veteran within the organization, deemed older and wiser than the hot-headed project manager and the death march volunteers who still have the stamina to work 18-hour days for months on end.

Bottom line: A project champion is more important than the latest methodology or razzle-dazzle programming language. A death march project without a champion to defend the team's disregard for bureaucratic rules and to support the team's decision to use risky techniques and technology is a lonely, miserable experience. I don't recommend it. If your champion is also the project owner, *and* if there aren't any other shareholders to worry about, *and* if your owner/champion is persuasive enough and involved enough to deal with the stakeholders, then you may have the luxury of ignoring all of these political issues. But unfortunately, most death march projects don't have that luxury; while it's usually the project manager who takes on most of the burden of dealing with the situation, everyone else on the team needs to be at least minimally aware of the cast of political characters.

2.2 DETERMINING THE BASIC NATURE OF THE PROJECT

In the previous chapter, I described several characteristics of death march projects: They can be big or small; they can involve one homogeneous set of customers or an incompatible, heterogeneous group; and, they can be affected by different combinations of schedule, budget, and resource constraints.

But, there's another way of characterizing these projects, and it's likely to have a significant political impact on all concerned. As illustrated in Figure 2.1, there are two key issues that can be mapped onto a two-dimensional grid; the horizontal axis represents the chances that the project will succeed, while the vertical axis represents the satisfaction or happiness that the project team members feel while the project continues. One way of determining where the team members would place themselves on the vertical axis is to ask, "When this project is over, would you consider taking on another death march project?" Or, more simply, "Are you in pain?"

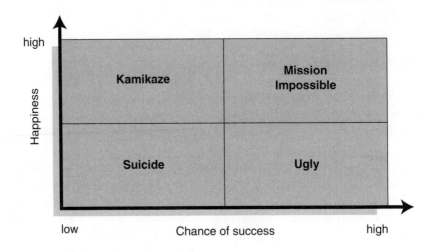

FIGURE 2.1 THE DEATH MARCH PROJECT STYLE QUADRANT

There's no particular scale on this chart, and the boundaries between the four quadrants are rather arbitrary; even so, I have yet to find a death march project that can't identify which quadrant they're in (though they may not have thought about it before I ask the question and draw the picture for them). It's highly doubtful that anyone initiated the death march project with the explicit intention of placing it into a specific place on the chart, but the combination of politics and project constraints (budget, schedule, etc.) will push the project in one direction or the other.

The descriptions of the four quadrants are also rather arbitrary, and you should feel free to change them to fit your organization's cultural idiosyncrasies. Here are the basic characteristics of the four quadrants:

- *Mission Impossible projects*—this is the kind of project glorified by the old TV series and the new (vintage 1996) Tom Cruise movie. The odds are heavily stacked against the project succeeding, and there are all manner of villains and traitors plotting the demise of the team. But, the project manager is a handsome Hollywood hero, the technical hackers are clever geniuses, and the team has God on its side. The team members are fanatically loyal to one another (notwithstanding the twist in the Tom Cruise movie), and it's clear that each individual thrives on the challenge and thrill of"living on the edge." And, while it's rarely indicated in the old TV series, the real-world mission impossible project teams typically do dream of fame, glory, and riches if they succeed. And, their mission *is* to succeed; they are convinced that a combination of hard work and technical virtuosity will make that possible.

- *Ugly projects*—these are the projects whose team members are sacrificial lambs that will be slaughtered by a cold-blooded project manager to bring the project to a successful end. Projects of this kind usually have the"Marine Corps"mentality discussed in Chapter 1—e.g., the project manager will be constantly haranguing his or her team that, "*Real* programmers don't need sleep!" The implication is also that "real" programmers don't have to go home to visit their families, nor do they have to visit their aging parents in the hospital, nor do they have to do anything else that would distract them for a moment from the demands of the project. In projects like this, it's not uncommon to see one or two of the project team members collapse from exhaustion, suffer ulcers or a nervous breakdown, or experience a divorce. And when it happens, the project manager chuckles, and tells the other team members that the unfortunate victim is a weakling who deserved his or her fate.

  The key characteristics of the ugly project are that (a) the project manager is determined to succeed, (b) the project manager is determined to survive, and thus profit from the success of the project, and (c) the project manager is willing to (and indeed *expects* to) sacrifice the health and happiness of the project team members to succeed.

- *Suicide projects*—in these projects, everyone is doomed, and everyone is miserable. The team members *and* the project manager have typically agreed to work on the project only because the alternative is being fired; and they know from the outset that there is no chance at all of succeeding. They can't afford to quit, they have no project champion, they have all the cards stacked against them...

- *Kamikaze projects*—these projects are doomed too, but everyone agrees that it will be a glorious failure, and one they will be proud to be associated with. The technical members of the project team sometimes derive their happiness from the opportunity to work with advanced technology they've never used before, and which they assume they'll never see again after the project collapses. The project manager hopes that the project will be an inspirational lesson to future project managers. Sometimes, kamikaze projects are associated with a doomed company whose glorious past has created such fierce loyalty on the part of the team members that they feel it is an honor and a privilege to be allowed to sacrifice themselves in a doomed project whose failure will be the company's last hurrah. Of course, there is a small chance that the project *will* succeed, and the company *may* survive; and even if the project team members utterly destroy themselves in the course of bringing about such a miracle, they will feel good about it.

From the comments above, you can probably tell that I'm in favor of mission impossible projects, and I admire kamikaze projects; I sympathize with those who have ended up on suicide projects; and I detest ugly projects. But that's *my* value system, and it may not be the same as yours. More important, it may not be the same as your project manager's value system; or, if you *are* the project manager, you may find that your value system is different than that of your team members'. For obvious reasons, it's a good idea to have everyone in the same quadrant. It's difficult to succeed with a mission impossible project if one or two key members think they're on a suicide mission.

Also, remember that public assurances from the various shareholders, stakeholders, and miscellaneous managers surrounding the death march project may or may not be honest indications of the *real* situation. One would like to hope that a project owner would not create a suicide-mission-style of death march project, but stranger things have happened in big companies—it may be part of a larger political battle that the project owner is fighting. Quite often, senior management has a broader scope of information which provides a more realistic picture of the project's chances of success. Your Vice President, for example, may be fully aware that a merger/acquisition is going to be publicly announced a week before the deadline of your death march project, and your project is going to be canceled at that point, no matter how well or poorly it's doing. C'est la vie.

The most common danger, though, is getting involved with an ugly-style death march project, in which the project manager refuses to acknowledge that he/she plans to sacrifice team members whenever it's expedient. Fortunately, it's usually easy to spot these situations, even when the manager refuses to acknowledge it. The "macho" behavior, and the denigrating references to weakling team members who can't keep up with the performance of "real programmers" are dead give-aways to the manager's attitude. Obviously, if you have a "Marine Corps" mentality, and are both willing and able to meet any physical, emotional, political, and psychological demands, then this won't matter to you.

Managers of ugly-style death march projects are often brought in from the outside, either at the beginning of the project or after the first project manager has quit or been fired. The new manager often has no past history or personal relationship with anyone in the company, and thus has less hesitation than might be expected when pushing the team members to work harder and longer. Indeed, I've seen several situations where the project manager is a "hired gun" who moves from company to company to take on the challenge of such projects. The manager typically delivers a successful project result—that's why he or she has got the reputation that allows him or her to charge hefty consulting fees—but the project team members are so disgusted and exhausted that they all quit at the end of the project (if not before), and the project manager has made so many enemies that he or she, too, has no choice but to pack his or her bags and move on to the next death march project. It's a perfect role for Clint Eastwood, and it's a situation to watch out for if someone bearing his likeness rides into town to take over the death march project you've just signed up for [5].

The best time to deal with these issues is *before* the project begins; as part of choosing the team members, the project manager should provide an assessment of what kind of death march project he or she expects it to be, and then ask prospective team members (a) how they assess the project, and (b) how they feel about occupying one of the quadrants in the diagram above. As I'll discuss in Chapter 4, I feel very strongly that the manager of a death march project *must* have the freedom of choosing the members of his or her team; and in addition to choosing the appropriate technical skills, it's also crucial to choose individuals who have a compatible assessment of the "style" of the project.

The situation is different, of course, if you're a prospective member of a death march project team, and you're being interviewed by the project manager. As discussed in Chapter 1, sometimes you don't have a choice about participating in the project, and contrary to the advice given in the previous paragraph, sometimes the project manager doesn't have a choice about whether to accept you as a member of the team; in this case, it's at least helpful to know how your manager assesses the project. If you *do* have the option of saying "No, thanks!" to the death march project, then it's all the more important to ensure that your assessment of the project is compatible with that of your manager. As discussed above, it's doubly important if your manager intends to carry out an ugly-style death march project; you need to ask yourself whether it's likely that you will be one of those sacrificed during the course of the project.

Remember also that the situation can change dynamically during the course of the project—because of the progress (or lack of progress) made by the team, because of the political situation outside the team, or because of physical or emotional exhaustion on the part of team members, etc.

2.3 IDENTIFYING THE LEVELS OF COMMITMENT OF PROJECT PARTICIPANTS

One last item needs to be discussed: the level of commitment the various project team members are willing and able to make to the project. To understand the notion of "commitment," recall the old parable about the argument between the chicken and the pig as to whose contribution to a bacon-and-eggs breakfast was most important.

"I work incredibly hard to produce those eggs each morning," the chicken says. "And they are the centerpiece of the breakfast meal."

"Well, there's no question that you're involved," replies the pig. "But I'm *committed*."

Paul Maskens responded to this parable with the following observation [6]:

> I'm not sure you will find any old pigs in development,
> perhaps more chickens. I think that kind of commit-
> ment continues until (inevitably?) you get into the first
> death march project—then there is a rude awakening.
> Either the pig realises what's happening, this is the
> slaughterhouse! RUN!! Or the pig is making bacon...

The level of commitment by team members is usually strongly influenced by the overall "style" of the project, as discussed above; for example, if everyone realizes they've been assigned to a suicide project, then they'll probably exert no more effort and emotion than absolutely necessary. And, even if management insists on large amounts of involuntary over-time during the project, you'll find that team members are spending evening hours and weekends (times when the high-level managers who imposed the overtime are virtually certain *not* to be present) catching up with personal phone calls, writing letters to their families, or sitting around the coffee machine shooting the breeze with one another.

Similarly, an ugly-style project will have a level of commitment dic-tated, or at least strongly influenced, by the demands of the project man-ager. My experience has been that the ugly-style project manager *is* willing and able to make the same level of physical and emotional com-mitment to the project that he or she is asking of everyone else; thus, if the project team is in the office on Saturday and Sunday, the ugly-style project manager will be cracking the whip over them.

But, what about the kamikaze- and mission impossible-style proj-ects? And, what about a death march project that nobody wants to char-acterize as being in one of the four quadrants suggested in Figure 2.1? In these situations, it's essential that the project manager get a realistic as-sessment of the limits that the team members have placed on their com-mitment to the project; and, for any of the project team members who are contemplating making an enormous sacrifice to their personal life for the next several months, it's important that they know whether they can ex-pect a similar level of commitment from their colleagues.

In the best of all cases, everyone will provide an honest assessment of their commitment and their constraints. "I'm 100 percent committed to this project," someone might say, "but my sister is getting married just before the deadline in June, and I'll be gone for three weeks, no matter what. I'm sorry the schedule worked out that way, but her wedding is the most important thing in my life." Since the rest of the project team doesn't even know the sister, this might be regarded as a frivolous excuse to disappear during the crucial final weeks of the project development effort—but at least the team member is being honest about his or her level of commitment [7].

Unfortunately, not everyone is able to announce a schedule of their personal commitments. A typical team member might promise a 100-percent commitment to the project, but if he or she has a child that has to be taken to the hospital, all bets are off. And of course, there's always the chance that a team member will win the grand prize in a lottery and receive a once-in-a-lifetime opportunity to take the entire family to Tahiti ... and who knows what other unpredictable events might pose a challenge to an otherwise sincere promise to devote oneself to the death march project on a 100-percent basis? [8] It's unrealistic to ask everyone to anticipate all the possible situations that might arise, but it *is* realistic for the project manager to provide an explicit and realistic picture of the level of commitment he or she expects from the team members. If a two-week absence to attend your sister's wedding is going to be considered an act of treason, far better to know about it in advance.

Brian Pioreck reminded me in a recent e-mail message that it's also crucial for the team members to be aware of each other's level of commitment, which the project manager can also accomplish through appropriate communication [9]:

> I think you also have to make their commitments public through the use of a project plan. Everyone sees the total involvement of all team members this way and what their own involvement means to the project. It is up to the project manager to communicate this and make their commitment match their effort.

2.4 SUMMARY

The discussion in this chapter doesn't provide any *operational* advice about managing, planning, or carrying out a death march project. But, style and substance are inextricably entwined in many aspects of life. Even if a death march project is following all of the "rules" about designing, coding, and testing a software system, the "style" issues discussed in this chapter can kill it.

Once we've identified the key players in the project, determined the "style" of the project, and communicated the level of commitment that the manager expects and the team members can realistically promise—then it's time to move on to the real work of the project. That begins with an even larger issue of politics: *negotiation*, which I'll discuss in Chapter 3.

Notes

1. Ed,
   >>Are there any other significant constituencies that I've missed?
   <<
   Yes. Developers, the people whose death is referred to in your title.
   >> How important do you think it is for _all_ of the project team members to be aware of the existence of these constituencies and whether or not they can be viewed as a "friend" or "foe" of the death march project? I personally believe that everyone on the team _should_ know this information, but I have manager friends who believe that this is too distracting, and that the developers should be spending every ounce of their energy on the project itself, while the project manager (who presumably is more politically adept) spends his or her time dealing with the outsiders. What's your opinion? <<
   I agree with your manager friends that the developers should be spending every ounce of energy on the project itself. But I also believe that information about each constituency is part of the project, so it's better for everyone (the constituencies, the managers, the developers) if the developers have that information. Any information that's relevant to the project but is hidden from the developers brings the project one step closer to the edge of failure.
   If the project manager were extremely talented at knowing what information was relevant, that might make a difference. I haven't

seen managers who were very good at that.

In general, I've observed that if there is a constituency whose input is relevant, the developers will often get it anyway, though perhaps in a more expensive, more distorted way than if the manager weren't trying to keep it from them. Other times, the developers will simply make assumptions about what each stakeholder needs.

>> mission impossible, kamikaze, ugly, suicide <<

I like these terms. I'm not sure how to know which kind of project I'm involved in until after the project succeeds/crashes. I think developers involved in a death march always believe (or are trying desperately to hold on to the belief) that they are in a mission impossible project.

>> How important do you think it is for the project manager to get a really good assessment of each team member's level of commitment? <<

"Level of commitment" is way too vague to be useful to me. If I am want to know what kind of "commitment" I can expect from someone, I would want to know what things in particular are more important to them than this project, and what things are less important.

I've always liked Watts Humphrey's ideas about "commitment discipline." He describes them in section 5.1 of "Managing the Software Process."

>> Is the project manager just kidding himself/herself by believing the team member's sincere statement of commitment, given that things can change drastically during the project? <<

Any statement of commitment can only describe how the team member feels right now, given what they know right now.

If a manager asking about commitment really wants to know, "How committed will you be, regardless of what happens on the project, regardless of what happens in our outside life, regardless of what demands I may make of you?" then any answer the team member gives is likely to be useless.

I've been asked many times to commit to achieving some result that is not completely within my control. I can tell you what actions I can commit to, but commit to a result and there are factors beyond my control, what would my statement of commitment do for you?

Dale

2. Ed,

>>1. Are there any other significant constituencies that I've missed? <<

In several of the death march projects I've experienced, I believe that there is a variation of shareholder that is very important to identify: the vendor, especially if they have people on site to

work on the project. Depending on who bought the project or
software from the vendor, you may have some difficulties right
away. A golf game sale for a package (my president plays golf with
your president) is a big predictor for a death march, since the
requirements process is typically shorted severely. Don't be the
first company to buy anything. Once the vendor staff and client
staff start banging heads, things rarely improve. It makes progress
that much slower since positioning and putting spin on project news
takes precedence over real project status. Makes it that much
harder to manage if you don't know who is telling you the truth or
when they are doing it.

- Dave

3. Ed,

<< [Stuff about identifying the key political players in a project]
Are there any other significant constituencies that I've missed? >>
Unfortunately, yes. You missed "the inner circle." These are the
people who have no direct stake in something yet they have
influence with those who do, an opinion on what should be done and
a burning need to inflict their opinion on others. Also known as
"the closest advisors," these people often spend time whispering
in the ears of decision makers in soft, subliminal tones and can
turn a friend into a foe overnight without you even knowing that
it happened. It happens in any political organization from the
White House to the Congress to any company with more than 3 people.
Even if they have no apparent stake, you had better have The Inner
Circle on your side if you want to make it. These people can be
old college buddies, the VP of Sales who has an opinion on
everything and the chutzpah to believe he is always right or the
faithful secretary of 20 years' service who has "seen it all" and
knows "what really works for us."

To put it another way, if you want to get anywhere with Mr. Clinton
you had better not make an enemy out of Mrs. Clinton.

<< How important do you think it is for all of the project team
members to be aware of the existence of these constituencies and
whether or not they can be viewed as a "friend" or "foe" of the
death-march project? >>

Essential. Yes, lot's of people hate getting into politics and want
to be left alone to "do their jobs." My response to that is, "It's
your job to get this software written, and these people can keep
you from doing that just as easily as any compiler fault or
hardware crash will. If you don't keep them happy, your job
evaporates."

<< I've identified four fundamental types of death march projects

in this chapter, from the perspective of the political climate that
will prevail during the project: >>
I've seen another type of death march, but it sort of screws up
your quadrant concept. I would call it "the lost squadron": We set
out to go somewhere, but the destination changed in mid-trip. And
then it changed direction again and again and again until finally
we started wandering around without knowing where we are or how to
get home. If we actually ever get finished it will only be because
we stumbled on the destination by accident.
<< How important do you think it is for the project manager to get
a really good assessment of each team member's level of commitment?
>>
Vital. Commitment breeds both efficiency and quality, and if you
can't get a reasonable handle on commitment, it makes estimation
and quality control that much harder.
<< Is the project manager just kidding himself/herself by believing
the team member's sincere statement of commitment, given that
things can change drastically during the project? >>
Probably. At the outset, every one tells you they are committed,
and they may even believe it themselves. The trick is to
continually re-assess the team members' commitment levels because
they will almost certainly change over time and thus the efficiency
and quality of death march work will change (almost certainly for
the worse) over time as well. It helps to be able to read minds <g>.
-Paul

4. For some reason, politicians (other than Bill Clinton) hate French fries, and seem to regard the odor as a direct challenge to their authority. I began noticing this on consulting engagements in the mid-1970s, when members of a project team I was working with told me in hushed tones that they had to keep the conference room door closed lest the highly feared Vice President smell the odor. I was delighted to see that Scott Adams remarked upon the problem in *The Dilbert Principle.* Could it be that university business schools are teaching MBAs that French fries are a Communist plot? Or, could it be that the managers most offended by the practice grew up before McDonald's started their enterprise in the mid-1950s, and never got over their rage at having missed out on one of the important American childhood experiences?

5. One such manager, whom I observed operating in the Wall Street financial services community, did have an interesting strategy for calibrating the physical stamina and emotional strength of his team: He would create a "false crisis" at the beginning of the project and *immediately* throw the entire team into a double-overtime level of effort. Then, he would stand back and watch to see what happened; one or two of the team members might quit, one or two might have a nervous breakdown, and one or two "quiet heroes" might emerge to solve the artificial crisis through hard work or a clever technical strategy. Having thus calibrated his team, the cold-blooded manager would then relax the pressure and get on with the real work of the project—confident that once the *real* crises began to occur (which they inevitably will in a death march project), he would have a good understanding of how his team would behave.

6. >> How important do you think it is for the project manager to get
   a really good assessment of each team member's level of commitment?
   << I'm not sure you will find any old pigs in development, perhaps
   more chickens.
   I think that kind of commitment continues until (inevitably?) you
   get into the first death march project - then there is a rude
   awakening.
   Either the pig realises what's happening, this is the
   slaughterhouse! RUN!!
   Or the pig is making bacon...
   To my mind this fits in quite nicely with the death march theme.
   Paul

7. The manager of an ugly-style project would probably pounce on this situation, and loudly complain that it was unacceptable. That's okay too—if it happens at the beginning of the project. The project team member is thus made aware of the need to make a binary choice; if the sister's wedding has the higher priority, it's better for the team member to resign gracefully at the beginning of the project than to be involved in an ugly personal crisis later on.

8. This is one good reason for having small project teams and short project schedules. A five-person team working on a six-month death march project is far less likely to be interrupted by unpredictable distractions than a 30-person team slaving away for three years. People *do* get married, they *do* have children, and they *do* have to attend to the other demands of a personal life; sometimes these events can be postponed for a few weeks or a few months, but it's almost impossible to block everything out of your life for three years.

9. Ed,
   >>1.... Are there any other significant constituencies that I've
   missed?<<
   I also include anyone who might be affected/involved by the
   implementation of the project. People who are not exactly
   stakeholders but whose cooperation is required for success. Say,
   the DBA group for example.

>>2. How important do you think it is for _all_ of the project team members to be aware of the existence of these constituencies and whether or not they can be viewed as a "friend" or "foe" of the death march project?<<

It is critical to developing the kind of group consciousness among team members that helps to compress time during a project. It will help the requirements process to be more accurate, cut down on the number of meetings required, and deliver better information from the meeting you do have.

>>...I have manager friends who believe that this is too distracting, and that the developers should be spending every ounce of their energy on the project itself, while the project manager (who presumably is more politically adept) spends his or her time dealing with the outsiders.<<

The whole concept of "outsiders" has to be abolished. It feeds the myth that developers are some kind of different family of the human species. Without the other team members involvement the developers could be spending every ounce of their energy building a project that is off target.

>>3. I've identified four fundamental types of death march projects...

The premise is that none of these are worthwhile outcomes right? I think it would be interesting to present these types without any death march explanation and let people pick which type of project they'd be willing to work on. The point is that so many projects are like these and people are so used to them they might not even question the categories.

>>4. ...How important do you think it is for the project manager to get a really good assessment of each team member's level of commitment?<<

It is critical. Without commitment you don't really have a project. Why is this person involved? What are they hoping to get out of this project? I think you also have to make their commitments public through the use of a project plan. Everyone sees the total involvement of all team members this way and what their own involvement means to the project. It is up to the project manager to communicate this and make their commitment match their effort.

--Brian

3
chapter

NEGOTIATIONS

A bargain is in its very essence a *hostile* transaction . . . do not all men try to abate the price of all they buy? I contend that a bargain even between brethren is a declaration of war.

Lord Byron, Letter, July 14, 1821
(in *Byron's Letters and Journals,* vol. 8)

If you're the manager of a death march project, it's very easy to predict the outcome of negotiations over budget, schedule, and resources: *you lose.* This is almost inevitable, because such negotiations take place at the beginning of the project (or even before the project if formally initiated), when the project owner/customer has neither the intellectual ability, emotional stamina, or political need to accept the unpleasant counter-offers being offered by the project manager. More rational negotiations sometimes take place a month or two before the deadline, when the first project manager has quit or been fired, and when a new project manager demands (as a condition of accepting the assignment) that everyone face up to the reality that the original deadline, budget, and required functionality will never be achieved.

Not one of us seems willing to accept this sad state of affairs. Thus, even though this chapter probably *could* focus on rational negotiating strategies for the replacement project manager, I'll nevertheless confront the question most of us wrestle with: How can we negotiate a tolerable set of conditions at the *beginning* of a death march project? Alas, there are no magic secrets to be revealed in this chapter; the dismal reality is that at the end of the process, you lose. Still, it's useful to be aware of the devious political games by which you're likely to be outmaneuvered, as well as the options that should be explored when you have been presented with a completely unrealistic schedule, budget, and/or staffing constraint.

My assumption throughout this chapter is that *you* are the one involved in the negotiations about death march projects, schedules, etc. If you're a technical staff member, you may be indirectly involved—e.g., by providing advice and estimating data to the project manager, so that he or she can carry out the negotiating battles with higher levels of management. But, in an e-mail communication with Doug Scott [1] recently, I was reminded that in some projects, even the project manager has but an indirect role, because all of the negotiations are being made on his or her behalf by the next higher-up manager:

> ...my biggest single obstacle in deathwatch projects has been my own management. I came to the UK in 1972, and moved on to big projects almost immediately. I don't think I learnt anything about running projects since that date (I learnt a lot about politics, but that's something else). You need to understand your own management's negotiating stance, and if they love to play roll over, you have to keep them well away from the project.

3.1 RATIONAL NEGOTIATIONS

The suggestion that we really *do* know how to accurately estimate the required schedule, budget, and resources for a non-trivial project will set up an emotional debate among any group of software professionals and managers. Our track record over the years certainly hasn't been a very good one; on the other hand, many would argue that the problems have been the result of political games associated with the very death march projects that we're discussing in this book. But, most large organizations can point to dozens of projects where the software team made its own schedule, proposed its own budget, and expressed supreme confidence that it would deliver a fully functional system within those constraints; the team then proceeded to hoist itself on its own petard and failed to deliver anything, at any time. So, it's no wonder that in many of these organizations, the user community and senior management have given up on the negotiating process, and have instead begun imposing "do-or-die" deadlines and budgets. Such is the genesis of many a death march project.

Still, that doesn't mean that we should abandon all efforts to derive a "rational" estimate that we can use in the preliminary negotiations for a project. Indeed, it's crucial that the project manager beware the temptation to give up and simply accept the initial death march project constraint as an edict. One of the common signs that a project team has adopted what I called a "suicide-style" behavior in Chapter 2 is the attitude—expressed by the project manager and echoed by the team members—that "we have no idea how long this project will really take, and it doesn't matter, since they've already told us the deadline. So we'll just work seven days a week, 24 hours a day, until we drop from exhaustion. They can whip us and beat us, but we can't do any more than that..."

I'm not going to discuss estimating techniques at length in this book; if the project manager has no skill or experience in estimating, then a death march project is no place to begin learning. But let me point out some of the obvious resources that we have available in this field:

- *Commercial estimating tools*—products such as SLIM, ESTIMACS, and CHECKPOINT are available from Quantitative Systems Management, Computer Associates, and Software Productivity

Research (SPR), respectively. SPR's Chairman, metrics guru Capers Jones, estimates that there are some 50 commercial project estimating tools. None of them are perfect, and all of them require intelligence on the part of the user (garbage-in/garbage-out applies in this field, too!), but in the best case, they can produce estimates that are accurate to within ± 10%. Even if they're only accurate to within ± 50%, it's better than the political demands that the project manager is coping with—which are often 1,000% beyond the ability of the team to deliver.

- *Systems dynamics models*—numerous simulation models have been developed to explore the non-linear interactions between various factors that affect a project's behavior. For example, if part of the strategy of a death march project is to impose a demand for heavy overtime on the part of the project manager, what will be the effects over a period of weeks or months? The natural assumption is that more "output" will be produced than would be the case with a normal eight-hour workday; but, most experienced project managers will also point out that productivity (measured in function-points per day, or lines of code per hour, etc.) gradually decreases as exhaustion builds up. Error rates also begin to increase, which has an obvious impact on the testing and debugging effort. And, if the overtime continues long enough, the project team eventually collapses from exhaustion. Of the simulation models that I've seen in this area, the best is Tarek Abdel-Hamid's [2], which has been implemented in languages like DYNAMO and iThink.

- Dozens of articles and books have been written on the topic of project estimating. Barry Boehm's *Software Engineering Economics* [3] is a good place to begin; it's important to note that Boehm's COCOMO model from the early 1980s has been updated to COCOMO-2 [4]. Another classic is Fred Brooks' *The Mythical Man-Month* [5]; this has also been updated recently, to reflect modern technology and software practices. A more recent book on software estimating is Jim McCarthy's *Dynamics of Systems Development* [6].

- The *process* of estimation has been studied and documented, and organizations like the Software Engineering Institute have published useful guidelines and checklists for improving the process of estimation [7, 8]. Even if we aren't very good at it, we know how to get better.

- Familiar techniques such as prototyping and time-boxing can be used to get an accurate picture of how feasible or infeasible the project constraints are for the overall system being developed. This is by no means a fool-proof approach, but it can inject a dose of reality into the project team and the surrounding layers of managers and customers. If management is demanding a system that will require a team of three to write a million lines of code in 12 months, then it should be possible to define a skeleton version of the system that can be built within the first month; this will provide at least a rough calibration of the team's level of productivity, as well as a rough idea of the overall feasibility of the project.

3.2 IDENTIFYING ACCEPTABLE TRADE-OFFS

Let's assume that the project team has prepared a "rational" estimate of the schedule, budget, and personnel required for a death march project; and let's assume that management is prepared for some kind of give-and-take process of negotiation before the final decisions are made. The most common situation is that management will declare the initial estimates "unacceptable" and make counter-demands that are far more stringent. What should the project manager do?

As author/consultant John Boddie [9] pointed out to me in a recent e-mail message, the crucial thing is to ensure that everyone agrees that there is more than one possible "scenario" for the project:

> Some useful questions during negotiations,
>
> "If the system is ready on the fifth of September rather than on the first, will we already have declared bankruptcy September second?"
>
> "Is there an 80/20 rule here? If we deliver the critical 20 percent that gives eighty percent of the value, do we need the twenty percent at initial roll-out?"

"Everybody wants things good, wants them fast, and wants them cheap. Everyone knows that you can actually achieve any two of the three. Which two do you want?"

The principle at work is to make those who are demanding the death march look unreasonable if they are unwilling to consider more than one possible outcome. Unless there is an acceptance of more than one way to approach the problem, then there is no negotiation. All the manager can say is, "We'll give it our best shot, but there are no guarantees."

If the counter-proposal from senior management or the customer involves only one "variable," the project manager can estimate the impact on the other variables. For example, if the manager's first estimate is that the project will take 12 months with three people and a budget of $200,000, it's possible that senior management's first response will be, "Baloney! We need to have that system up and running in *six* months!" The obvious way to accomplish this is to add more people and/or spend more money (e.g., pay higher salaries to hire more productive programmers).

But, Fred Brooks told us more than 20 years ago that the relationship between time and people on a software project is not a linear one; the term "man-month" (which would probably be expressed as "staff-month" in today's politically correct organizations) was thus exposed as a myth. Indeed, the relationship between *all* of the key variables in a project is likely to be non-linear, and it's likely to be time-sensitive as well. Because of the "feedback effect" of many management decisions, a change in one variable (such as adding more staff) will not only have an impact on other variables (such as productivity) over time, but will eventually have an impact on the original variable—e.g., the hiring of additional staff could lower morale, which in turn could raise the turnover rate within the project, and ultimately *reduce* the size of the staff.

The non-linear, time-sensitive nature of these interactions is the essence of the systems dynamics models mentioned above; but it's also the reason for using the various commercial estimating tools described earlier. There is a key point here: The mathematics behind the systems dynamics models are typically based on non-linear differential equations, and most of us aren't very good at doing that level of mathematics in our heads. Similarly, the commercial estimating tools carry out elaborate calculations involving dozens of parameters; trying to do this intuitively, based on a "gut" feeling for the situation, is likely to be quite error-prone.

Unfortunately, that's exactly the situation many death march project managers find themselves in. Sometimes this is because of the nature of the negotiating process (particularly a game called "Spanish Inquisition," which I'll discuss below); but, it's also caused by the lack of estimating tools and expertise in many organizations. Again, this is not a problem you're going to be able to solve in a death march project, if it hasn't been addressed already. If the organization is accustomed to deriving its project estimates by scribbling numbers on the back of an envelope, the death march project manager probably won't get away with spending $10,000 on a sophisticated estimating tool.

So, what should the manager do in a situation like this? In the extreme case, the manager should recognize the futility of the situation and respond appropriately; I'll discuss that in more detail in Section 3.5 below. But, in the less extreme case, here are two guidelines:

- If the negotiating demand from users or senior management involves a change of <10% in one project variable, then you can compensate by increasing one of the other variables in a direct, proportional fashion. Thus, if management wants the schedule reduced by 10%, then add 10% to the size of the project team. This isn't entirely accurate, but it's a good first-cut approximation, and it's often all you can get away with from a negotiating perspective.

- If the change involves more than 10% in one dimension, then you should assume it will have an "inverse square law" impact on any other single dimension. Thus, in the scenario above, management wants to cut the project schedule in half, 12 months to 6. Rather than responding by doubling the size of the project team, the manager should *quadruple* the team—or quadruple the budget, in order to hire superprogrammers who can code with both hands at the same time. Without a formal estimating model, there's no way to know whether this crude heuristic will be accurate for any specific

situation, but at least it's better than falling into the trap or negotiating a "linear" exchange of time for people. Unfortunately, the
inverse square law is difficult to negotiate, and there's a good
chance that the project manager's "outrageous" demands will be
beaten down; but with luck, the manager will still end up in a better position than the linear exchange would provide.

3.3 NEGOTIATING GAMES

Negotiating *is* a game, and it takes place on all software projects. What's
different about death march negotiations is that the stakes are much
higher, emotions are much more highly charged, and the demands of the
other side (in terms of schedule, budget, etc.) are usually so extreme that
they overwhelm any "safety factor" that we might have used in the past.
The most obvious safety factor in a traditional project, for example, is
overtime. Even if the project manager has been brow-beaten into a tight
schedule and restricted budget, success can still be achieved by asking
the project team to work 10 to 20 hours per week of overtime for the final
few months of the project. The additional effort doesn't show up in the
official records, because the programmers aren't paid for overtime work;
thus, the manager ends up looking like a hero.

But, in a death march project, modest amounts of overtime are typically inadequate to achieve the dramatic results that are being demanded. Besides, the users and senior management aren't naive—they *know* that
overtime effort can be requested, and they've factored that into their own
estimate of the "required" schedule for the project—thus pre-empting the
manager's opportunity to hide that free resource. But, project managers
who are veterans of such negotiations should have a few tricks up their
sleeves, which can be pulled out when the bargaining sessions begin.

The neophyte project manager is at a terrible disadvantage; in the extreme case, the neophyte isn't even aware that his past successes may have
occurred *only* because the project team voluntarily contributed sufficient
overtime effort to compensate for a ridiculous project schedule. And the ridiculous schedule may have been imposed upon the team precisely because of the manager's naiveté in the area of estimating negotiations.

Management consultant Rob Thomsett has described the most common negotiating games in a wonderful article [10]; I've summarized the more familiar games below:

- *Doubling and Add Some*—this is a ploy that has been used on projects dating back to the Pyramids, if not earlier. Use whatever estimating techniques you have available, then double the "rational" estimate; and, for added safety, add three months (or three weeks, or three years, depending on the overall size of the project). The major problem with this strategy is that it runs head-on into the most pressing constraint associated with death march projects: schedule compression.

- *Reverse Doubling*—as noted earlier, management hasn't been oblivious as software project managers have attempted to "pad" their estimates by the doubling strategy discussed above. One reason for this political astuteness is that the senior managers in many organizations today are former IS/IT project managers—so they're intimately familiar with the games involved. As a result, they take the initial estimates given to them by the project managers, and automatically cut them in half. Pity the poor neophyte project manager who doesn't realize that he or she is *supposed* to double his or her estimate at the outset!

- *"Guess the number I'm thinking of"*—this is a game I learned in one of my first projects, as a junior programmer. The user or senior manager has an "acceptable" figure for the schedule, budget, and/ or other aspects of the negotiation, *but refuses to articulate it.* When the project manager offers his or her estimate of schedule and budget, the user/senior manager simply shakes his or her head and says, "No." The implied message is, "That's too much—guess again." The hapless project manager eventually (sometimes after half a dozen attempts!) comes up with an acceptable estimate, but because it's *his* or *her* estimate, the user/senior manager is all the more determined to hold him or her accountable.

- *Double Dummy Spit*—"dummy" is Australian slang for a baby's pacifier, and "spit the dummy" is an Australian phrase describing a baby so frustrated and angry that it spits out its pacifier. Thomsett uses this as a metaphor to describe negotiating session when a senior manager erupts in a fit of rage when the project manager first makes his or her proposal for the death march project schedule and budget. The chastened manager scurries away, comes back with a revised estimate, and the senior manager erupts again— hence the "Double Dummy Spit." The idea is to get the manager so cowed and terrified that he or she will go along with anything, in order to avoid yet another temper tantrum

- *Spanish Inquisition*—this occurs when the project manager walks into a meeting of higher-level managers, completely unaware that he or she is going to be asked to make an "instant estimate" for the death march project. Imagine a roomful of grouchy Vice Presidents staring at you while the CEO asks you in thunderous tone, "So, Smithers, when do you expect to get the Frozzle System done? I've told the whole management team that we'll have it on-line by mid-March—you're not going to let me down, are you?" If you're brave enough to suggest that mid-November would be a more realistic estimate, you'll have a dozen inquisitors questioning your intellect, your credentials, your loyalty, and perhaps even your religious faith.

- *Low Bid*—with outsourcing an option in many organizations today, this game is becoming more and more common; it's also common in any situation where a software development organization is bidding against other competitors for the privilege of developing a system for a client organization. The game is obvious: The customer (or sometimes the development organization's marketing representative) tells the project manager that one of the other bidders has proposed a faster development schedule and/or a lower budget. This puts pressure on the project manager to not only match the competing bid (which may or may not be a "real" bid), but to improve upon it to raise the chances of getting the contract. A variation on this game occurs when the client lets it be known that he or she is considering the option of not doing the project at all; a software development organization that's desperate to get the approval to initiate the project (perhaps because it will advance the career of the IS/IT Vice President) will ensure that the project proposal is so attractive that it will be approved. Of course, this means that in many cases, one or more members of the IS/IT hierarchy *knows* that the project proposal is unrealistically optimistic, and perhaps even a blatant lie. This in turn leads to the "Gotcha" and "Chinese Water Torture" games described below.

- *Gotcha*—the "Gotcha" game is sometimes played by the project manager as a way of getting revenge: Though he or she knows at the outset that the project proposal is unrealistic, he or she accepts it anyway—on the theory that by the time everyone is forced to face up to reality (e.g., a week before the deadline), it will be too late for the client to back out. But, it's a dangerous game, because the client has to ask whether he or she wants to throw good money after bad. If the organization has a track record of previous projects running amok in this fashion, the client may decide to cancel the project and write off the expenses as a bad investment. But, chances are that the death march project *won't* be canceled right away, because it's usually associated with business objectives, legal requirements, or political battles that are difficult to walk away from. However, that doesn't prevent the customer from seeking revenge for having the game played on him, and the most obvious form of revenge is to fire the project manager. This is also a common political ploy for various higher-level managers and marketing representatives (who may have been responsible for the death march project commitments in the first place) to escape the problem of "guilt by association." Everyone can rationalize to themselves that the reason for the problem is the incompetence of the project manager; a new project manager is brought in, a more realistic set of revised project schedules and budgets may or may not be negotiated, and the project continues. Meanwhile, of course, nobody thinks to relax the pressure of overtime work on the technical staff members of the team.

- *Chinese Water Torture*—rather than facing a high risk, all-or-nothing showdown near the end of the project, another common game is to bring the bad news to the customer and/or higher management in small pieces. Imagine the scenario, for example, where the project manager's rational estimate for the project is 12 months; with forced overtime and lots of miracles, he thinks it might be possible to finish in 6 months, but management has imposed a 4-month deadline upon the project. Reluctantly, the manager concedes and announces a series of "inch-pebble" deliverables for the project—e.g., a new prototype version of the system will be delivered for customer review every week. The first deliverable turns out to be a day late, but the manager reasons that the delay represents 14 to 20% of the deadline for that deliverable (depending on whether the team is working a 5-day week or a 7-day week); thus, he or she argues that the deadline for the final version of the system should also be pushed back by 14 to 20%. Management refuses to concede any slippage at this early point, but when the second inch-pebble is also a day late (meaning a cumulative delay of two days over a period of two weeks), the manager repeats his or her argument. Drip, drip, drip; it's like Chinese water torture—no one single piece of bad news is enough to kill you, but the cumulative effect can be fatal.

- *Smoke and Mirrors*—Pity the poor project manager whose higher-level IS/IT Vice President has hired a metrics consultant with an estimating model that nobody understands. Software metrics are ultimately a form of statistics, and estimating models are based upon sophisticated mathematics. When put in the hands of the innocent, the naive, and/or the politically motivated, these tools can be used to "prove" the validity of almost any estimate. All of this is doubly dangerous if the metrics come from a vendor attempting to prove that the death march project will succeed because of the stupendous productivity of the vendor's CASE tools, visual programming language, or newfangled software engineering methodology.

- *Hidden Variables of Maintainability/Quality*—this is one of the more insidious games, and it can be played in a constructive or destructive fashion by knowledgeable project managers, higher-level IS/IT managers, and/or customers. It's very simple: As a project manager, I can deliver an infinite amount of software to the customer in zero time, *as long as it doesn't have to work and it doesn't have to be maintained*. Obviously, it would be foolish to propose a scenario this extreme, but the point is that quality (in the form of defects, portability, maintainability, etc.) is a project "dimension" that has to be taken into account when trade-offs are being considered between time, money, staffing, and other resources. Some customers are too naive to recognize this, and some of them have a very cold-blooded, short-term perspective: "I don't care if the system works two years from now, because I think the business opportunity will be gone—and in any case, I'll be gone. All I care about is that the system has to be available three months from now, and it has to work for 12 months after that." If the political pressure is strong enough, you may find IS/IT managers and the project manager adopting this attitude; it's far less common to see the technical staff members accepting it as a reasonable way of doing business. In the best of cases, this "game" represents the strategy of "good-enough" software that I described in my *Rise and Resurrection of the American Programmer* [11]; in the worst case, it's as dishonest and reprehensible as several of the other political games described above.

3.4 NEGOTIATING STRATEGIES

What should you do if you find yourself being sucked into one of the political games described above? Equally important, what should you do if you're an innocent bystander—e.g., a technical staff member of the project team—and you observe such games being played all around you as the project deadline, functionality, and budget are being negotiated? Thomsett makes the interesting point that we all learn these political games from our mentors, our managers, and the "elders" of the political culture in our organizations; thus, even if we can't escape the games ourselves, perhaps we can refuse to teach them to our subordinates, in the hope that the whole process of political games will die out after another generation of two.

It's a noble thought, but I'm not so optimistic. I sometimes think that political behavior is genetic, firmly imprinted on our DNA pattern. But even if it's not this bad, the reality is that political games of the nature described in this chapter are all around us; none of this is unique to software projects, and all of us have been exposed to variations on these games throughout our lives. Even if these games were unique to software projects, there's enough mobility within the software profession that an organization is almost certain to be "infected" by highly political managers, vendors, and marketing representatives over a period of time. Political games are something we have to accept as an unavoidable phenomenon, and we have to cope with them as best we can.

One thing we *can* do—and this also comes from Thomsett's excellent article—is to avoid getting sucked into the trap of producing an "instant estimate" for a project. The Spanish Inquisition game is the worst form of this, but there are many lesser forms that appear during the planning and negotiation stages of death march projects. Whether it's innocent or malicious, the project manager will often be asked for an instantaneous "rough estimate" for the time or staffing required for some aspect of the project; and once it's been blurted out in public, it often becomes a hard, unmovable requirement for the project. So, in any situation of this kind, the manager needs to respond with a statement like, "I'll need a day (or a week or a month—or even an hour!) to make some calculations before I can give you an estimate. I'll let you know by e-mail." There are obvious political advantages to being prepared in advance, so that you've already done the necessary calculations before you get hit with the questions; but, that's not always possible.

And it's not always possible to avoid the demand for an instant estimate. Suppose you're sitting in a marketing presentation, and the client turns to you and says, "Okay, Harriet, suppose we eliminate the interactive Web browser portion of the system, agree to do the whole thing on our in-house network, and add ten of our people to your project team. How long will it take you to get the job done?" All eyes turn to you, and you can see the marketing manager squirming; you probably know from all the discussions that have led up to this question that the politically acceptable answer is, "Three months—no problem!" What are the chances that you will be able to say, "Gee, I don't really know; we'll have to go back to the office and run that through our estimating model. And I'd also have to interview your ten people to see what their skills are..."

In a situation like this—and even many of the situations where you *do* have some time to put together a formal estimate—it's crucial to state your estimates in terms of "confidence levels," or a "plus-or-minus" range. If you have absolutely no data with which to construct a detailed estimate, and if the death march project involves completely new technology, and unknown people, then it might be prudent to say, "The project will probably take between three and six months," or "I think we can finish in six months, plus-or-minus 50%."

Of course, most project managers are aware of this technique, and they may or may not be using it already. Deciding how large or small the "plus-or-minus" range should be is part of the science of estimating, and I'll leave that to the textbooks listed at the end of this chapter. For death march projects, it's important to keep in mind the *politics* of stating confidence levels during the negotiating process. The most basic political reality, for example, is that anything you say about a plus-or-minus range will be ignored by everyone else that you're negotiating with. Thus, if you're sitting in a planning session and you tell the customer and various other senior managers, "We should be able to get this project done in six months ±25%," everyone will write down "six months" on their note pad [12]. No matter how many times you say it, they'll ignore it; and when your boss feeds the information back to you, you'll find that your deadline is six months. The only thing you can do is *never* drop the plus-or-minus qualifier in *any* verbal or written statements, promises, commitments, or estimates that you provide. It won't eliminate the problem, but it will provide an excuse if the project ends up at the high end of your estimate.

Unfortunately, there's an uglier aspect of the political negotiation when you introduce the plus-or-minus qualifier into your estimate: You'll be accused of uncertainty, wishy-washiness, weakness, or even incompetence. This is particularly common in the "Marine Corps" style of death march projects discussed earlier. What senior management really wants is a firm commitment—a *promise* that the project will be finished on a certain deadline, with a budget of a certain number of dollars, and a staff of a certain size. This gives them the enormous luxury of (a) no longer having to worry about the problem for the duration of the project, and (b) having a convenient scapegoat to blame if the promise is broken. An estimate that takes the form of "X months ± 50%, for $500,000 ± 100%, and with 10 people ± 25%" eliminates that luxury.

Jim McCarthy, in his excellent book *Dynamics of Software Development* [13], suggests that the project manager needs to confront this head-on, and persuade the customer and/or senior management that they need to share some of the burden of uncertainty that the entire project team will be living with on a day-to-day basis. Thus, the project manager effectively says to the customer or the senior management group, "Look, I *don't know* precisely when this project will finish—but since I'm the project manager, I'm far more likely than anyone else in the organization to figure it out as soon as it *can* be figured out. I promise you that once I know, I'll tell you right away."

Only a manager with a lot of self-confidence, *and* the ability to walk away from the assignment, can have the chutzpah to say something like this in the politically charged atmosphere of a death march project. But, the time to say it is at the beginning of the project; after all, if the customer and senior management don't respect your ability as a project manager, and that you *do* have a better chance of knowing when the project will finish than anyone else, then why are they putting you in charge of the project in the first place? Are you being set up as a scapegoat? Are you going to be a "puppet manager," with all the decisions being made by other political manipulators in the organization? If so, now is the time to get out!

Similarly, if you're a lowly programmer on the project team and you see political games like this, it may be a strong indication that your project manager (a) doesn't have the confidence to believe in any estimate that he or she puts forth, (b) doesn't have the backbone to stand up for himself or herself and for the project team, and/or (c) has gotten himself or herself into a political situation where all the key decisions are going to be made by people who are not directly involved in the project. Again, this is a strong indication that the project is doomed; and before you get too deeply involved, it might be a better idea to seek greener pastures.

Having said this, I'm nevertheless well aware that it's extremely difficult for the project manager to persuade the various "players" to share the uncertainty of the project schedule, budget, and staffing decisions. A savvy customer will indeed do this; a sophisticated IS/IT organization will recognize all of this as an aspect of risk management, which needs to be carried out in a blameless political environment; and human beings who care about and respect one another will agree that it's unfair to make one member of a group carry the ulcer-generating pressure of a high-risk situation.

3.5 WHAT TO DO WHEN NEGOTIATING FAILS

In the discussion above, I suggested that if the project manager couldn't persuade the customer or senior management to share some of the uncertainty associated with the schedule or budget of a death march project, he or she should seriously consider resigning from the assignment; the same goes for technical members of the project team. But, this is only one aspect of a "failed" negotiating process; what should the manager do, for example, if he or she is 100% certain that the politically mandated deadline of six months cannot and will not be achieved? What should he or she do if he or she is 100% certain that the project must have a minimum of three people, but management will only provide two?

I've mentioned the option of resigning a few times already in this book, and I realize that it's not a practical option for some software professionals; indeed, it's more likely to be a problem for project managers than the technicians, for the simple reason that project managers tend to be 5 to 10 years older, and thus saddled with the impediments of mortgages, dependent family members, half-vested pension plans, etc. They also tend to be a little more insecure about their chances of getting another job quickly, while the younger, unmarried project team members are typically much more confident that they can land another job within 24 hours.

It's important to realize here that I'm not recommending resignation as a form of punishment or revenge. It's simply the rational thing to do when faced with an impossible situation, and implacable negotiating adversaries. Life will go on; there will be other projects; and there will be other jobs. As Sue Peterson remarked to me in a recent e-mail message [14]:

> I've learned something from my kids, and I think it applies to work just as much as it does to home life... I *have* to protect myself, my energy level, my emotional and physical health, my quiet-time, and my work time. If I don't protect myself, I won't have anything left for them anyway.

But, there's another issue associated with quitting that needs to be confronted here: the issue of loyalty and the "social contract" between

employer and employee. Up through the 1980s, many software professionals worked in large organizations whose corporate culture involved
an assumption of a "job for life." While it was never as strict or as explicit
as in Japanese companies, most programmers and software engineers at
major banks, insurance companies, government agencies, and computer
companies (like IBM and DEC) assumed that in the absence of war, fam-
ine, or plague, they would continue to rise through the organization until
they finally retired at age 65, with a gold watch.

Small companies have never had this kind of culture, and many software professionals *have* worked for small companies, especially as computer technology has become cheap enough that even a Mom-and-Pop
grocery store could afford a PC and Web server. And, those of us who
have worked for consulting firms, service bureaus, and various forms of
entrepreneurial, high-tech start-up companies have always known that
there is no such thing as a lifetime social contract.

Software professionals in large companies have begun to learn this
too, because the era of downsizing, outsourcing, and reengineering has
caused major disruptions and unemployment in our field. This has been
exacerbated by mergers and acquisitions in the computer field, and also
in highly competitive industries where information processing is a major
part of the work-force. When Chemical Bank and Chase Manhattan
Bank merged a couple of years ago, for example, senior management had
to deal with the problem of merging two entirely different hardware environments, systems environments, and IS/IT management hierarchy.
And, as I mentioned in Chapter 1, it's *exactly* this kind of situation that
has led to many of the death march projects that have been taking place
all during the 1990s.

The problem in many of these large organizations is that while the
employ*er* has definitely changed the social contract, the employ*ee* has
not reacted accordingly. Many software engineers who have put in 10
or 20 years of loyal service still assume that (a) the company will take
care of them, and (b) they should stand by the company, no matter
how unpleasant it might be. And "unpleasant" is the operative term
for most death march projects. It's not fun sacrificing all of your spare
time, working to the point of exhaustion, and coping with stress and
political tension. So why do we do it? Because we've signed on for life,

and we feel that ethical people should honor their commitments.

However, if the employer has invalidated the social contract, then all bets are off; it's crucial to re-evaluate the relationship and see whether it's worth continuing at all. I certainly don't advocate unethical, immoral, or even amoral behavior—but I see nothing wrong with limiting my commitment to an employer to a period of a year or two, or for the extent of a single project. An employer that says to the death march project, "Get this system finished by December 31 or you're fired," is essentially articulating the same kind of "short-term" social contract.

The threat of being fired—which certainly does occur in death march project negotiations—is only one form of "hard-ball" negotiating; threats of being bypassed for a raise or promotion are also common. But if the social contract has been abandoned, and if you're dealing with a "hard-ball" negotiator in a death march project, then you have the right to play "hard-ball" too. And, one of the strongest bargaining chips in a negotiating session is your adversary's [15] recognition that you're ready and willing to walk away from the relationship if the results aren't mutually acceptable.

If senior management threatens to fire you if the death march project fails, or if you don't accept the unrealistic deadline they've imposed upon you (which may be two different ways of saying the same thing), you should be equally cold-blooded in your demands. You may not get them to budge on the deadline, but you can probably be much more demanding than otherwise possible when it comes to staffing your project (I'll discuss this in more detail in the next chapter). And, you can *definitely* be more cold-blooded when it comes to ignoring or breaking the administrative and bureaucratic rules and procedures that would otherwise guarantee failure for the death march project.

A variation on this is the old adage of, "act first, apologize later." It may be a waste of time to "negotiate" a reprieve from the various bureaucratic restrictions that you've decided will ham-string your project. It's certainly worth attempting to do so, because an edict from a high-level manager will usually give you sufficient authority to circumvent or ignore the minions of administrators, committees, and standards-enforcers that will swarm around the project. But, if you get a wishy-washy answer—

e.g., "Well, we're not sure it's a good idea for your programmers to move off-site and have two PCs in their office; we'll check with the Building Services Committee and see what they think"—then stop wasting your time. Just go ahead and do it!

If you're clever, you can probably find a way to circumvent many of the bureaucratic obstacles in such a way that it will take six months for the bureaucracy to notice, and to mount an offensive; by then, your project may have finished (or failed) anyway. And, if the bureaucracy does mount an offensive, be prepared to play hard-ball; after all, your project is now well under-way, and management probably can't afford the risk that you (and the entire project team) will walk out the door and force the project to be re-started. There are two points to keep in mind if you choose this approach:

- You have to be prepared to have your bluff called. If the Methodology Police visit your project and throw a tantrum because you're not using the company's official methodology, you may well get a furious phone call from your boss's boss's boss. You need to be prepared to say, "Mr./Ms. BigShot, we've decided not to use the methodology because it will guarantee failure. If you feel strongly about this, my team and I are prepared to resign today—otherwise, I'd appreciate it if you would leave us alone, and tell the Methodology Police to leave us alone, too. We have work to do." *This won't work unless the senior manager truly believes that you and your team _will_ resign on the spot, if pressed.*

- You must be prepared to deal with enemies who will hold a grudge, even if your project succeeds. In the scenario above, you've challenged the authority of the BigShot manager; he or she won't forget it. You've embarrassed the Methodology Police, and made it more difficult to impose their methodology on other victims; they won't forgive you. Indeed, you may have burned so many bridges that at the end of the project, you (and perhaps the rest of the team too) will be so unpopular that you'll have to quit.

If resignation and "hard-ball" negotiating isn't an option on your death march project, then what should you do if the negotiating process yields unsatisfactory results? Very simple: re-define the nature of the project, as suggested in Figure 2.1 (Chapter 2). In the early stages of negotiation, you may have thought you were beginning a mission impossible project. In fact, given adequate resources and a talented staff, you might have been prepared to accomplish miracles. But, if you're given inadequate resources and brain-dead programmers, then miracles are not going to occur.

Indeed, it's more likely that you're being pushed into a kamikaze or suicide project; only as a variation of the "hard-ball" negotiating process described above could we imagine that the outcome would be the ugly style of project described in Chapter 2. In any case, the key point here is that the project manager must believe in the possibility of achieving the project goals (e.g., deadline, required functionality, etc.), and the manager must be able to convince the team members of the viability of those goals without "conning" them. As John Boddie [16] points out in a superb book on managing "crunch-mode" software projects:

> The project leader who cares about his people will not try to sell them a bill of goods about the project. He will be honest about the level of effort it will require and its chances of success. Programmers aren't stupid. The experienced ones will have a keenly developed sense to tell them when they're being "fed a line." Most of them won't be a party to project games because they know they are the ones who will shoulder the burden when the crunch comes.

And, if the project manager has determined that the death march project goals are *not* viable, but the project must continue anyway, then it's crucial that the manager explain to the staff members that they are signing on for a suicide or kamikaze mission. Some will accept the mission anyway, and it's important for the manager to understand what their reasons are [17]; but, others will resign.

There's an interesting aspect of ethics here. As noted earlier, I don't advocate unethical or immoral behavior, but I also believe that the negotiations surrounding a death march project almost always force the project manager to deal with the owner/customer and/or senior management as an adversary. The members of the project team, on the other hand, are like one's family. More than just treating the team members ethically and professionally, the manager should feel the responsibility of "taking care" of the team, to ensure that they don't become innocent victims in the political battles. I'm indebted to John Boddie [18] for tracking down a maxim from Napoleon that expresses this thought more eloquently than I could on my own:

> It follows that any commander in chief who undertakes to carry out a plan which he considers defective is at fault; he must put forth his reasons, insist on the plan being changed, and finally tender his resignation rather than be the instrument of his army's downfall.

Napoleon, *Military Maxims and Thoughts*

Notes

1. Ed,
```
> I'm going to be suggesting in this next chapter that the project
> manager be sure to identify .....
> Are there any other significant constituencies that I've missed?
```
I think simply identifying them is a good first step, and then you need to understand why they would want the project to succeed. Many don't care, and could thus get in the way. Opponents will stick out like a sore thumb.
But my biggest single obstacle in death watch projects has been my own management. I came to the UK in 1972, and moved on to big projects almost immediately. I don't think I learnt anything about running projects since that date (I learnt a lot about politics, but that's something else). You need to understand your own management's negotiating stance, and if they love to play roll over, you have to keep them well away from the project.
```
> 2. How important do you think it is for _all_ of the project team
> members to be aware of the existence of these constituencies and
> whether or not they can be viewed as a "friend" or "foe" of the
> death march project?
```
This has to be managed. In any project, having an external focus to push against does help to solidify a team. But you mustn't allow this to stop them helping you. If you need this, I'd say you need to keep it to single individuals. Death march projects, because of their size and importance, will usually attract hostility from surrounding people anyway, so it won't be too difficult to create

an enemy - the trick will be to make sure that your potential
helpers aren't all enemies as well.
> *   mission impossible: if we succeed, we live happily ever
after
Done that. I don't think I ever classified it as a deathmarch, in
the way I'd normally think of one. But I did develop an ulcer,
so... <g>
> *   kamikaze: the project may succeed, but it will kill all
of us
Dunno. The certain death is so demotivating, I'm not sure if people
would continue. They'd probably rationalise it into another type
of project.
> *   ugly: the project manager is prepared to sacrifice any
>   and all of the team members in order to succeed.
Well, I think this comes with the territory. It's part of being a
death march.
> *   suicide: the project has no chance of success, and we're
the scapegoats
Yes, this seems to be one of the fears with death marches.
I don't think I can go along with your matrix, in this case. True
death marches have some characteristics - there is a (possibly
remote) possibility of success; it's so tightly time-boxed that
success within the timescales is difficult to imagine, and one of
the pastimes is to watch announced deadlines being slipped while
still being aware of the need for further slippage.
Personal satisfaction is never high on a deathmarch, and the chance
of success is low - I guess that's what defines a death march. Most
death marches fall into your suicide category, I'm afraid. If you
had high personal satisfaction and high anticipation of success
(which I reckon are correlated anyway), that's not a deathmarch.
As I say, I believe the true differentiator lies in the timescale,
rather than in personal feelings. If the timescale is impossible,
then you *know* you're on a deathmarch. The only question then is
whether you die expensively or slowly.
> How important do you think it is for the project manager to get a
 > really good assessment of each team member's level of
commitment?
If anyone asks me that question nowadays, I know to run a mile,
because that PM will turn the project into a death march. I've
never had trouble getting people committed, once I've set up an
environment where that commitment will pay results. But I have seen
many environments where overtime is regarded as more important than
what you're doing (a friend who's just joined Oracle is replete

with that attitude now), and I'm not at all impressed by their
output.
> _negotiations_. I'll deal with that in Chapter 3
Let me know. when you need stories here. Many are so unbelievable
that it's not worth even telling (such as "I don't mind you
refusing changes to the design even if it is a fixed price project
- all I have to do is ring your chairman, and he'll always tell
you do it.").
--Doug (back on OS/2 and GCP)

2. Tarek Abdel-Hamid and Stuart Madnick, *Software Project Dynamics* (Englewood Cliffs, NJ: Prentice-Hall, 1993).

3. Barry Boehm, *Software Engineering Economics* (Englewood Cliffs, NJ: Prentice-Hall, 1981).

4. Barry Boehm, Bradford Clark, Ellis Horowitz, Chris Westland, Ray Madachy, and Richard Selby, "The COCOMO 2.0 Software Cost Estimation Model," *American Programmer*, July 1996.

5. Frederick Brooks, *The Mythical Man-Month*, 20th anniversary edition, (Reading, MA: Addison-Wesley, 1995).

6. Jim McCarthy, *Dynamics of Software Development* (Redmond, WA: Microsoft Press, 1995).

7. Robert E. Park, Wolfhart B. Goethert, and J. Todd Webb, *Software Cost and Schedule Estimating: A Process Improvement Initiative.* Technical Report CMU/SEI-94-SR-03 (Pittsburgh, PA: Software Engineering Institute, May 1994).

8. Robert E. Park, *Checklists and Criteria for Evaluating the Cost and Schedule Estimating Capabilities of Software Organizations.* Technical Report CMU/SEI-95-SR-005 (Pittsburgh, PA: Software Engineering Institute, January 1995).

9. Ed,
re: if you know of any good negotiating strategies (other than
blackmail and torture, which I can't recommend in a book like this
<g>), let me know.
The only leverage that the manager has is to bring the risk of
failure out into the open and as publicly as possible start
postulating fallback positions.
Some useful questions during negotiations,
"If the system is ready on the fifth of September rather than on
the first, will we already have declared bankruptcy September
second?"

```
"Is there an 80/20 rule here? If we deliver the critical 20 percent
that gives eighty percent of the value, do we need the twenty
percent at initial roll-out?"
"Everybody wants things good, wants them fast, and wants them
cheap. Everyone knows that you can actually achieve any two of the
three. Which two do you want?"
The principle at work is to make those who are demanding the death
march look unreasonable if they are unwilling to consider more than
one possible outcome. Unless there is an acceptance of more than
one way to approach the problem, then there is no negotiation. All
the manager can say is, "We'll give it our best shot, but there
are no guarantees."
--JB
```

10. Rob Thomsett, "Double Dummy Spit and Other Estimating Games," *American Programmer*, June 1996.

11. *Rise and Resurrection of the American Programmer*, Edward Yourdon (Upper Saddle River, NJ: Prentice Hall, 1996).

12. Actually, the politically astute people will take your worst-case estimate and add another "safety factor" before reporting it to their next higher-level superior. Your estimate of six months, ±25% thus becomes nine months or a year. Unfortunately, the politically naive, or the politically ambitious, will do just the opposite. Thus, the CEO may end up being told that your project will be done in four months or less.

13. See Note 6, above.

14. Ed,
```
>>Another important question I want to discuss in this chapter:
what should the death-march project manager do when, in his/her
sincere opinion, the negotiations have failed? At what point does
the manager resign, throw a tantrum, threaten to become the next
Unabomber, etc.? And when he/she reaches that stage, what
responsibility does he/she have to the project team, which may have
already begun working? <<
I've learned something from my kids, and I think it applies to work
just as much as it does to home life... I _have_ to protect myself,
my energy level, my emotional and physical health, my quiet-time,
and my work time. If I don't protect myself, I won't have anything
left for them anyway.
--Sue P
```

15. Some readers will probably object to the notion of the customer, or one's senior manager, being described as an "adversary." But, the very nature of a death march project is that the owner/customer, and the various shareholders and stakeholders, are consciously and deliberately pushing the manager into decisions that he or she would not make on his or her own. And, if you don't think that "adversary" is an appropriate characterization of someone with whom you've had a warm, friendly, professional relationship for years—go back to the beginning of the chapter and read Lord Byron's comment again.

16. John Boddie, *Crunch Mode* (Englewood Cliffs: Prentice Hall/Yourdon Press, 1987).

17. It's possible, for example, that a disgruntled staff member may see the death march project as an excellent way of wreaking revenge upon the organization—and he or she may join the project team in order to make *certain* that the project fails.

18. See Note 16.

PEOPLE IN DEATH MARCH PROJECTS

When soldiers have been baptized in the fire of a battle-field, they have all one rank in my eyes.

Napoleon Bonaparte, Quoted in: Ralph Waldo Emerson,
Representative Men, "Napoleon" (1850)

A general is just as good or just as bad as the troops under his command make him.

Douglas MacArthur, Speech, August 16, 1962

Insist on the right to choose your own team. Expect the team to work some overtime hours, but remember that they're on a marathon, and they should only be expected to sprint for the final 100 yards. Reward them handsomely if the project succeeds, but don't dangle extravagant awards in front of them all through the project, for it will distract them. Focus on building a loyal, cohesive, cooperative team; it's important to have the necessary technical skills, but it's even more important to have complementary psychological constraints. That's all there is to success-fully integrating peopleware in a software project.

Unfortunately, there's more to it for many death march project man-agers, for they work in organizations that have a miserable peopleware culture even for normal projects. Though it might seem that such a cul-ture would doom a death march project to certain failure, it sometimes turns out that just the opposite is true. As noted in Chapter 3, the project manager may have to accept an unreasonable schedule or budget, but can sometimes retaliate by being equally hard-nosed about various peo-pleware issues. Thus, the manager might insist on—and get away with—the right to hire the right people for the team, reward them properly, and provide them with adequate working conditions.

And, for precisely that reason, the death march project will be perceived as a threat to those who want to maintain the bureaucratic status quo. The project manager may be able to circumvent the peopleware restrictions with an edict from senior management, but he or she must be aware that in doing so, he or she will earn the permanent enmity of the Office Police, Hu-man Resources department, and various administrators. However, if the death march project is a tremendous success, it may prove to be a catalyst to change the peopleware practices for subsequent "normal" projects.

In any case, my mission in this chapter is not to change the overall peopleware culture in an organization. Much has already been written about this, including chapters in my *Rise and Resurrection of the American Programmer* and *Decline and Fall of the American Programmer* (I've also provided a list of standard references at the end of this chapter). The basic question addressed by this chapter is: If you're already familiar with the "basics" of peopleware, what's different about a death march project?

4.1 HIRING AND STAFFING ISSUES

The first thing that's different about a death march project is the empha-sis on forming the right team. In my work with software organizations around the world, I've seen four common strategies for creating a death march team:

- Hire superstars and turn them loose

- Insist on a well-honed, mission impossible team that has worked together before
- Choose mere mortals, but make sure they know what they're getting in for
- Take whoever you're given and convert them into a mission impossible team

The first strategy is tempting, because the presumption is that the superstars will be enormously productive, and also clever enough to invent novel solutions to the death march requirements. However, it's also a risky strategy, because the superstars typically have super-large egos, and may not work well together. And, it's impractical in many organizations, because management isn't willing to pay the higher salaries demanded by the superstars. And, even if you *could* afford them, chances are they wouldn't be willing to work on the death march project—they're all working at Netscape or Microsoft, or wherever they think the really exciting projects are taking place.

The second strategy is almost certainly the ideal one for most organizations, because it doesn't require superstars; it's also the kind of project team glorified by the *Mission Impossible* TV series. However, if your organization is embarking upon its first death march project, such a team doesn't exist. And, if there were previous death march projects that turned out to be suicide-, kamikaze-, or ugly-style projects, the teams are probably no longer intact. Thus, a strategy of keeping a *successful* death march project team intact usually must be planned in advance, as a corporate strategy, on the assumption that death march projects will occur again in the future (I'll discuss this in more detail in Chapter 7).

The third strategy is the most common in the organizations I visit, for obvious reasons. Most organizations have no superstars, and they have no survivors from previous death march projects. Hence, each new death march project is staffed anew. The team members are competent, and perhaps better than the average developers in the organization, but they can't be expected to perform miracles. What's vital in this scenario is that the team members understand what they're signing up for; even though they're mere mortals, they will be called upon to perform extraordinary feats of software development.

The final strategy is one to be avoided at all costs. If the project turns out to be a dumping ground for personnel that no other project wants, then it's almost certainly a suicide project. Again, this has been glorified by Hollywood, especially in movies like *The Dirty Dozen*; the theme is that outcasts and misfits can be motivated by a tough, charismatic leader to perform miracles that nobody thought possible. Well, perhaps so, but Hollywood doesn't tell us about all of the misfit-staffed projects that fail. It seems to me that if you accept the assignment of managing (or participating in) a project of this kind, you've accepted the fate of suicide.

This brings up the central issue of staffing the death march project team: To what extent should the project manager insist on the right to make the staffing decisions? As noted above, most project managers have to accept the fact that they won't be given *carte blanche* to hire the world's most talented superstars; and, politics within the organization may make it impossible for the project manager to steal away the best people within the organization, because they're already involved in other critical projects, or fiercely defended by other managers. Nevertheless, there is one aspect that I believe the manager should insist on, as an absolute right: the right to *veto* an attempt by other managers to stick an unacceptable person onto the team. To do otherwise is to add an unacceptable level of risk to a project that's probably already over-burdened with other risks.

Obviously, this can lead to a variety of ugly political battles. The project manager is likely to hear soothing statements like, "Don't worry, Charlie has been having some problems on previous projects, but he'll be fine on your project," or ego-boosting statements like, "You're such a terrific manager that I'm sure you'll be able to turn Charlie around and get some real productivity out of him," or various appeals to loyalty, bravery, and assorted Boy Scout-like virtues. My advice is to stand firm and insist on the right to reject anyone that you don't think will fit well into the team.

One of the criteria that should be used in such a decision is the likelihood of the proposed staff member leaving before the project finishes. Obviously, most software developers won't tell you if they're planning to quit midway through the project; but, some of them *will* tell you about anticipated personal priorities—marriage, divorce, a prolonged mountain-climbing expedition to the Himalayas, etc.—that could rule them out of consideration. In general, it's crucial to avoid losing people in the midst of a death march project; and, it's highly desirable to avoid having to add new people in the middle of a project.

In Chapter 3, I discussed the options available to the project manager if negotiations fail: quit, appeal to a higher authority, ignore the rules and make your own decisions, or redefine the project as a suicide mission. The possibility of ignoring the rules is usually more difficult, because adding extra personnel to the project team has payroll ramifications that are beyond the manager's control. However, it *is* sometimes possible to "borrow" people from another project, or perhaps even to hire some temporary contractors.

It's also possible to isolate an unacceptable team member that has been put onto the project against the manager's wishes; the unacceptable team member can be given a harmless sub-project to work on, or sent away to research the mating habits of African tsetse flies until the project is finished. Doug Scott [1] described an even more elaborate version of this strategy in a recent e-mail message to me:

> Death Marches often end up in the desperate situation where senior management will throw money at you— "You want another twenty people?" And I always accept. I put the bozos onto manning the coffee machine, changing fuses, and other essential work, while I hang on to the better ones. (Randomly, you will get a few good ones). Then you can assist the bozos to resign and keep pressing for more and more people to replace them. In one case, I cut to 20% of the original staffing level, and still maintained work output—but the quality of that output was excellent. That's no surprise to anybody, but it's by constantly demanding more resources and losing them that you can achieve it.

4.2 LOYALTY, COMMITMENT, MOTIVATION, AND REWARDS

I discussed the issue of *commitment* to the death march project in Chapter 2; it's an essential element of the politics of such projects, and it's also a key element in the team dynamics that the project manager must try to maximize. Ideally (from the project manager's perspective), the team members will swear an oath of loyalty and dedication to the death march project above all else; for the young, unmarried techno-nerds, this is not as ridiculous as it might sound. However, it depends heavily on such things as the length of the project. Total devotion may be feasible for a three to six month project, but probably not for a 36-month project.

Commitment also depends heavily on the ability of the project manager to motivate the team members to *feel* loyal and committed. To some extent, this is a matter of charisma. Some managers generate such feelings of loyalty that their team members will follow them to the end of the earth, no matter how risky the project; other managers are so uninspiring that their teams wouldn't exert any extra effort, even if the project's objectives were to save mankind from an alien invasion.

Of course, one could argue that the project manager shouldn't allow anyone to join the team unless they *are* highly motivated. One could also argue that the issue is irrelevant, because most software developers are already motivated—as Tom DeMarco and Tim Lister argue in *Peopleware* [2]:

> There is nothing more discouraging to any worker than the sense that his own motivation is inadequate and has to be "supplemented" by that of the boss... You seldom need to take Draconian measures to keep your people working; most of them love their work.

But, there are levels, or degrees, of motivation. We might expect a software developer to exhibit a certain degree of motivation for a normal project, but death march projects demand a higher degree of motivation to sustain the team members through months of exhausting work, political pressure, and technical difficulties. And, the project manager faces the practical difficulty of not knowing just how motivated the team members are when the project begins. As Doug Scott [3] puts it:

> You're assuming that he knows who these people are
> when he gets them. I've usually had them assigned to
> me before I know how good/bad they are.

In many cases, the biggest factors in motivation/de-motivation will revolve around the dynamics of the overall team (I'll discuss this in more detail below). But, there are two specific issues that also have a significant impact on motivation, and which are usually under the manager's direct control: rewards and overtime.

4.2.1 Rewarding Project Team Members

Things would be difficult enough if we could solve the motivation problem by dangling large sums of money in front of all of the project team members (and the manager, too!). But, Frederick Herzberg [4] suggests that money is not always the answer:

> Money, benefits, comfort, and so on are "hygiene"
> factors—they create dissatisfaction if they're absent,
> but they don't make people feel good about their jobs
> and give them the needed internal generator. What
> does produce the generator are recognition of
> achievement, pride in doing a good job, more respon-
> sibility, advancement, and personal growth. The secret
> is job enrichment.

This may be an accurate assessment for normal projects, but money does play a factor in many death march projects. Indeed, it may be an overriding objective for the project as a whole. Many Silicon Valley start-up companies embark upon frantic death march projects, hoping that they will be able to develop a "killer app" for a new hardware device and sell millions of copies to an eager marketplace. If the project team members have stock options and profit-sharing plans, financial rewards are obviously a very large part of the motivational structure of the project. Indeed, many Silicon Valley companies deliberately peg their salaries at 20-30% below the prevailing market rates, but provide ample stock options and/or profit-sharing plans to motivate the members of their technical staff. The strategy is not only to increase motivation, but also to reduce the fledgling company's cash outflow, since salaries are often the single biggest expenditure for a start-up software company.

Of course, there *are* legitimate, exciting death march projects for which money is irrelevant. A software developer who is offered the once-in-a-lifetime chance to work on the equivalent of the Apollo 11 lunar landing doesn't need money; he or she will cheerfully agree with Steve Jobs' comment about the Macintosh project that "The journey is the reward."

At the other extreme, I find death march projects taking place in moribund government agencies where the project is intrinsically boring, and where there is no hope of increased financial reward for *anyone* in the organization. Salaries are determined by one's civil-service grade-level, and the salary structure is fixed by law—there are no bonuses, profit-sharing rewards, or stock options. In cases like these, it's obviously silly to even discuss financial rewards as a motivator—all it can do is frustrate the team.

But, what about the organizations that have flexibility? If the death march project is important enough to the organization, then it's not beyond the realm of possibility to set aside a significant bonus pool to reward the team if it succeeds in delivering the project on time. The possibility of bonuses comes up in normal projects too, but the monies involved are usually much more modest. It's nice to get a bonus check of $1,000 at the end of a normal project, but the tax authorities usually take a third for themselves, and the remainder is not enough to have a noticeable impact on the lifestyle of a typical middle-income software professional. But, death march projects are different: a $10,000 bonus check might be enough to buy a new car (albeit a pretty modest one these days!), or finance a vacation to Bali. A $100,000 bonus check is enough to finance a child's Ivy League college education, or to buy a house (or at least the down payment on a house). And, a $1,000,000 bonus check is enough to make retirement a serious possibility.

Assuming that such a bonus is possible, here are a few observations:

- Remember that a 20% salary increase means much more to a junior programmer earning $25,000 per year than it does to a senior programmer making $75,000 per year. At the higher salary, the marginal tax rate is usually much higher, often approaching 50%; thus, the programmer doesn't take home much more, and consequently the salary issue is more likely to be regarded as a hygiene factor. For the junior programmer though, the tax rate is still reasonably low, and the extra 20% might be sufficient to cover the monthly payments on the programmer's first car, or to justify moving out of his/her parents' home to an apartment.

- Remember that the possibility of large sums of money can motivate people in a variety of ways. Management may assume that it will simply make everyone work harder, but it can also make team members excessively critical and suspicious of each other—e.g., a team member will complain bitterly, "George had the audacity to take Christmas Eve off, just to be with his stupid family, right when we were at a critical stage of testing. He's gonna screw us out of our bonus!"

- Remember that the size of the bonus doesn't have a direct, linear correlation with the productivity or number of hours worked by the project team. I've watched senior management in some organizations attempt to bribe the death march project team by offering to double the size of the bonus—usually because the project is behind schedule, and because management apparently believes that doubling the bonus will double the number of work hours by the project team. But, if the team members are already working 18 hours per day, the laws of physics prevent even the most dedicated person to double the work hours.

- For the bonus to work as a motivator, the project team must believe that it really exists and that senior management won't find a devious excuse to withhold it. Obviously, if the rewards are associated with success in the marketplace—e.g., if the project succeeds, then the company can go public, unless the stock market has collapsed—there are no guarantees. But, if the reward is entirely at the discretion of senior management, and if the team believes that previous death march project teams have been unjustly cheated out of their rewards, the "promise" of a bonus will probably be a *negative* motivator. Similarly, if the project team concludes that it has little control over the successful outcome of the project—e.g., because, in addition to their software, the project depends on new hardware being developed by an outside vendor—they may view the bonus being promised by management as a "random lottery," rather than as a motivating device.

- The team must also believe that the bonus will be distributed in an equitable fashion. That doesn't necessarily mean that every team member gets exactly the same share; but, if the team believes that the project manager will get the lion's share of the reward, and that they'll end up with the crumbs, the results are predictable. This needs to be discussed at the beginning of the project; it's unlikely that the team members will be pacified by statements from the manager like, "Trust me, don't worry—I'll make sure everyone is taken care of in a fair manner."

For projects that cannot or will not consider extravagant bonuses, it's important for the project manager to remember that there is a wide variety of non-financial rewards that can have an enormous impact on the motivation of the project staff. Again, this is an issue that we frequently see on "normal" projects, but it's more important here because everyone is being stretched to his or her limits. It's also important to remember that the pressure of the death march project team is felt by the spouse and/or family members of the death march staffers. As Doug Scott puts it [5],

> The first priority is to take pressure off your staff, so the first recipient of the rewards should be to the partner and family of said staff—it's all very well in career/ money terms, but it's the family who have to make the sacrifices. Bouquets of flowers are a start. Support the whole family—they're the ones doing it.

While a bouquet of flowers is a nice gesture, it's sometimes more meaningful to provide "practical" rewards to the family members—especially the spouse who is left juggling all of the household and child-care responsibilities while his or her "significant other" is working 'round the clock on the death march project. A thoughtful project manager might check to see whether the spouse needs a taxi service to pick up or drop off a child from school, or whether someone from the office could pick up some groceries on the way home to help the spouse who is stuck at home with sick children. And, if the children are *really* sick and need medical attention, the project manager will move heaven and earth—and utterly destroy any bureaucratic obstacles—to ensure that the appropriate services are provided, in order to minimize anxiety on the part of the death march project member.

Of course, the examples mentioned above *do* require money, but it's usually a very small amount of money, and it can usually be covered in the "miscellaneous" part of the project budget. Again, the corporate bureaucrats will probably whine and complain if they find out about it, for such expenditures usually don't conform to officially sanctioned procedures. The project manager who caves in to this kind of pressure is a spineless wimp; if necessary, the manager should pay for such expenses out of his own pocket, since he's usually making a much higher salary than the technical staff members. In any case, it's the manager's job to deal with the corporate bureaucracy here; the last thing we want is to have the technical staffers wasting their time and their emotional energy fighting with the accounting department about whether it was reasonable to order a pizza with two extra toppings, rather than the economy pizza, for a midnight dinner when the team is working late.

Modest rewards of this kind throughout the project will certainly help; but, what about non-financial rewards of a more lasting nature when the project finishes? I'm not thinking of promotions or new career opportunities here, for those fall into the same category as overt financial rewards. Here are some examples of rewards that might not be quite as motivating as a million-dollar bonus check, but would nevertheless help ease the pain of a death march project:

- *An extended vacation*—if the project succeeds, give the team members a vacation of the same duration as the project. Most of us aren't quite sure what to do with a two-week vacation—but if we had a six-month *paid* vacation, it might motivate us to take that 'round-the-world sailing trip we've always dreamed of. An interesting test: Try this idea out on your manager and watch the reaction. If it's something like, "What?!? Are you nuts? Six months vacation for a six-month death march project?!? We'll give you a couple days off, but don't push your luck!" it will give you a strong indication of management's implicit belief that software developers are nothing more than indentured servants. Such an attitude speaks volumes about the organization's concept of a social contract.

- *A paid sabbatical*—when the death march project is done, assign the team members to a six-month stint on "Project X" [6]. Question: What's "X"? Answer: Anything they want it to be. Rather than immediately being assigned to another death march project (or equally bad, an utterly boring non-death march project), the team members can look forward to six months of learning about Java, researching the latest object-oriented methodologies, or even returning to college to get their Master's degree. You'll have to be a little creative about the "official" name for X to confuse the bureaucrats; something like "the advanced nimbo-heuristic, object-oriented, Internet-savvy, Java-based, strategic-forecasting client-server system" might do the trick.

- *A fully-equipped computing environment at home*—even though PC hardware has gotten much cheaper and we all have something set up in our home office, it's usually not the most up-to-date equipment. Many of us have a sluggish 486-, or even an ancient 386-based machine, while the rest of the world races ahead to 200 MHz Pentium machines. The interesting thing about death march projects is that they often accumulate extra computer equipment, because management is prepared to throw extravagant sums of money into the budget on the theory that advanced technology will save the project. If there is leftover equipment at the end of the project, give it to the team members as a bonus; if an outright gift breaks too many bureaucratic rules, then loan it to them.

4.2.2 The Issue of Overtime

If bonuses and extended vacations are a motivator, then overtime during the project would normally be considered a "de-motivator." But, it's almost inevitable on death march projects; indeed, it's usually the *only* way that the project manager has any hope of achieving the tight deadline for the project. And, as noted earlier, it often occurs without any explicit requests from the manager: young, fanatical, unmarried team members who are excited by the challenge and advanced technology associated with the project will happily work 60, 80, or 100 hours per week.

Nevertheless, overtime must be managed properly to avoid demotivating the team and endangering the success of the project. One way to manage overtime is to ensure that senior management knows how much it costs; as consultant Dave Kleist puts it [7],

> Unless stock options for the company are distributed to team members as generously to senior management, there are no forms of compensation for a death march that would qualify as a reward (I'm using reward as a term with a positive tone). While the PM rarely has this control over compensation, what really should be done is immediate compensated overtime in the next paycheck. This gives something back to the people sacrificing the most for the project, and punishes (through the budget) the people who need to learn the real cost of a project (senior management, etc).
>
> If you're going to do a deathmarch, it's best to get paid by the mile.

Regardless of whether or not the team members are being compensated for their overtime work, the worst mistake is not recording the overtime, on the theory that since the team members aren't being paid for it, it's "free." While this may be an accurate perception on the part of the accounting department, overtime is *not* free from the project manager's perspective. Even if we assumed that all team members could work 18-hour days forever, without ever becoming tired, it's crucial for the manager to keep track of how many "invisible" overtime hours are being contributed throughout the project. This is the only way the manager can accurately gauge the productivity of the team and the likelihood of reaching each mini-deadline throughout the project.

And, as everyone knows, people can't work 18-hour days forever; even if they try, they get tired. When they get tired, they get cranky and short-tempered, they work less productively, and they make many more mistakes. All of this has a dramatic impact on the progress of the overall project, and the manager has to know when to relax the pressure, and when to ask for more overtime.

This may not seem so important for a three to six month project, when a young, energetic project team can work "flat-out" from beginning to end. But, on longer projects, careful management of the overtime effort is crucial; the effects of long periods of heavy overtime are insidious, but nevertheless quite real. As Doug Scott suggested to me in a recent e-mail message [8]:

> Part of scheduling deliveries is to ensure that the overtime comes in bursts and is then allowed to diminish - you can't keep people working at 90% and over for very long.

And as John Boddie, [9] points out, it's important that the manager recognize that each team member will have a different tolerance for overtime work:

> Individuals have different metabolisms. Some are night people, others work better in the early morning. Irrespective of type, nobody's health is going to be ruined by working ten-hour days. Once the project gets rolling, you should expect members to be putting in at least 60 hours per week. If they're not, check first to see if there's something in the way the project is organized that's frustrating them.

> The project leader must expect to put in as many hours as possible. This is done for two reasons. First, he must provide an example. You cannot expect people to work overtime if you're not doing it yourself. Overtime must be led. Second, he must be there to answer questions, cut through red tape, and fix problems that come up during odd hours.

One of the dangers that the project manager must watch for is excessive *voluntary* overtime on the part of enthusiastic young software engineers who don't know their own limits, and who don't appreciate the potential side-effects of working when they're exhausted. As suggested by Figure 4.1, net productivity might actually *increase* during the first 20 hours of overtime work, based on adrenaline, concentration, etc. But sooner or later, everyone reaches a point of diminishing returns; and at some point, productivity begins to decline because of increased errors and lack of focus and concentration. Indeed, there comes a point where the team member becomes a "net negative producer," because the re-work effort caused by mistakes and defects exceeds the positive contribu-tion of new software developed. Thus, assuming that the scale in Figure 4.1 is accurate (which it may or may not be, for any individual software developer), the manager will probably want to encourage the developer to work as much as 60 hours per week; the period between 60 and 80 hours per week is where the manager should begin letting the developer set his or her own limits; and beyond 80-90 hours per week, the manager should insist that the developer go home and rest.

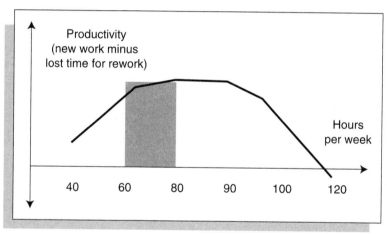

Note that the shape of this curve depends on age, motivation, and length of the overall project

FIGURE 4.1 NET PRODUCTIVITY VS. HOURS WORKED

4.3 THE IMPORTANCE OF COMMUNICATION

One of the important peopleware issues for death march projects is the nature and extent of communications between the project manager and the rest of the team. In my opinion, the ideal situation is one where the project manager has no secrets—everyone on the team knows everything about the project. This means that *everyone* on the team knows the *current* information about the project status, priorities, risks, constraints, politics, etc.

One reason for suggesting this is that it builds trust and loyalty among team members. If the team members are making extraordinary personal sacrifices on behalf of the project, it's very disillusioning to discover that the project manager has been withholding crucial information, or has been playing political games behind the backs of the project team members. And because death march projects tend to be intense and fast-moving, there's more of a chance than in normal projects that the team members *will* find out that information has been withheld, or that political shenanigans are going on.

The obvious counter-argument to this philosophy is that the project manager should be buffering the team from distractions—especially the petty political games that surround the project on a day-to-day basis. And in most cases, the team members will appreciate being spared all of the politics; but, they also need to know that if they ask a direct question, their project manager won't obfuscate or lie to them. In most projects, normal or death march, there's a regular status meeting where questions of this kind can be raised; if the staff members are satisfied that they can find out what's going on whenever they need to, they'll be happy to concentrate 99% of their energy on their technical work.

Communication *between* team members is also crucial, especially in the unfortunate situation where the team members have not worked together before. It's crucial that intra-team communication be kept confidential (from outsiders) to encourage honest and frank exchanges of information. For most projects today, this strongly implies the need for electronic mail and various forms of groupware along the lines of Lotus Notes. But in addition, the project manager should plan for weekly lunch, beer, or dinner sessions so that the staff members can interact with one another outside the normal office environment.

4.4 TEAM-BUILDING ISSUES

Open, honest communications are an important ingredient in the process of building an effective team. Choosing individuals who are compatible with one another is another key ingredient. As mentioned earlier, it's crucial that the project manager have the freedom to choose his or her team members, and it can be helpful to use techniques such as Briggs-Meyers personality assessment tests to help anticipate how team members will interact with one another.

Yet another ingredient involves the concept of team *roles*. Many project managers focus on "technical" roles such as database designers, network specialists, user-interface experts, and so forth. But while these roles are important, it's also important to think about the "psychological" roles that will be played by one or more team members. These roles are visible in "normal" software projects too, but they are all the more crucial in death march projects. Rob Thomsett [10] has described the eight key project roles as follows:

- *Chairman*—controls the way in which a team moves forward toward the group objectives by making the best use of team resources, recognizes where the team's strengths and weaknesses lie, and ensures that the best use is made of each team member's potential. As might be imagined, this person is often the official project leader; but in self-managing teams, it could be any one of the individuals.

- *Shaper*—shapes the way in which the team effort is applied, and directs attention and seeks to impose some shape or pattern on group discussion and on the outcome of group activities. This individual may have the official title of "architect" or "lead designer," but the key point is that it's a "visionary" role. Especially in a death march project, it's crucial to have a single, clear focus on what the problem is, and what the solution (design) should be.

- *Plant*—advances new ideas and strategies with special attention to major issues, and looks for possible new approaches to the problems with which the group is confronted. I like to think of this person as the "provocateur"—the person who introduces somewhat radical ideas and technologies into the group, to help find innovative solutions to help solve the technical problems confronting the death march team.

- *Monitor-Evaluator*—analyzes problems in a practical manner, and evaluates ideas and suggestions so that the team is better placed to make balanced decisions. In many cases, this person acts as the "skeptic" or "critic," thus balancing the optimistic proposals of the shaper and plant. The monitor-evaluator is aware that new technologies don't always work, vendor promises about the features of new tools and languages are sometimes broken, and things in general don't always go as planned.

- *Company Worker*—turns concepts and plans into practical working procedures, and carries out agreed-upon plans systematically and efficiently. In other words, while the shaper is spouting grand technological visions, the plant is proposing radical new solutions, and the monitor-evaluator is looking for the flaws and shortcomings in those proposals, the company worker is the person who hunkers down in a corner and churns out tons of code. Clearly, a death march project needs to have at least a couple of these folks; but on their own, they may not bring the project to success because they don't have any grand visions of their own.

- *Team Worker*—supports members in their strengths (e.g., building on suggestions), underpins members in their shortcomings, improves communications between members, and generally fosters team spirit. In other words, this person is the "diplomat" of the team. It may be the project manager, but it could also be any one of the individuals on the team who happens to be a little more sensitive than the others about bruised egos and sensitive personalities. Again, this is often a crucial role in death march projects, because the team is often under a great deal of stress, and at least one or two of the team members is likely to begin behaving in an insensitive, "macho" fashion.

- *Resource Investigator*—explores and reports on ideas, developments, and resources outside the group, creates external contacts that may be useful to the team, and conducts any subsequent negotiations. I like to call this person the "scavenger," because he or she knows where to find a spare PC, an available conference room, an extra desk, or almost any other resource that the team needs. Such resources might or might not be available through official channels; but even if they can be procured in the "normal" fashion, it often requires filling out 17 forms in triplicate and then waiting six months for the bureaucracy to process everything. A death march project can't wait that long, and can't afford to have all its progress brought to a halt because the Vice President's administrative assistant jealously guards access to the organization's only available conference room. The team scavenger often has a network of friends and contacts throughout the organization from whom the critical resources can be begged, borrowed, or stolen. The most important thing is that the scavenger *enjoys* this activity.

- *Completer*—ensures that the team is protected as far as possible from mistakes of both commission and omission, actively searches for aspects of work which need a more than usual degree of attention, and maintains a sense of urgency within the team. It's common to see this person taking on the dominant role during the testing activities at the end of the project life cycle, but it's just as important in the earlier stages too. The team sometimes needs to be reminded—daily!—that it's not involved in a lifetime career, but rather a project with a hard deadline, with intermediate inch-pebbles that need to be accomplished in a timely fashion to avoid falling behind.

Unfortunately, even with all this effort, there's no guarantee that the project team will come together, or "jell," in a cohesive fashion. As Tom DeMarco and Tim Lister put it in *Peopleware*:

> You can't make teams jell. You can hope they will jell; you can cross your fingers; you can act to improve the odds of jelling; but you can't make it happen. The process is much too fragile to be controlled.

If the jelling process is successful, there will usually be some visible signs. As DeMarco and Lister observe, successful teams typically have a strong sense of identity, a sense of eliteness, a feeling of joint ownership, and (at least on mission impossible-style death march projects) a feeling that they can do good work *and* have fun. On the other hand, while the organization may not be able to guarantee a successfully jelled team, it *can* cause what DeMarco and Lister refer to as "teamicide"—i.e., a conscious or unconscious decision to give up and abandon all efforts to maintain a focused, cohesive team structure. The practices that typically lead to teamicide are these:

- *Defensive management*—not trusting the team. Note that this is an area where the notion of a team "champion," as discussed in Chapter 2, becomes essential.

- *Bureaucracy*—too much paperwork. If the team has any sense, it will simply refuse to do the paperwork, or will make vague promises to catch up with all of it after the project has finished.

- *Physical separation of team members*—(e.g., in different buildings, different cities, different countries)—electronic mail and groupware tools can obviously reduce this problem, but physical proximity is essential to maintain the team spirit so essential to the success of a death march project.

- *Fragmentation of people's time*—especially in situations where the team members devote part of their time to the official death march project, and another part of their time maintaining an old legacy system, or serving on the committee for the company Christmas party. It's mind-boggling to imagine that such a thing could happen in a death march project, but it *does* happen in large corporate bureaucracies.

- *Quality reduction of the product*—while the team may be prepared to accept a certain level of quality-reduction in order to deliver "good-enough" software on time, there is usually a threshold below which they refuse to go. The quality issue may involve defects (bugs), missing functionality, primitive user interface, or shoddy documentation.

- *Phony deadlines*—for example, deadlines so aggressive that the team has absolutely no faith in its ability to meet them. This form of teamicide usually transforms a mission impossible team into a suicide team.

- *Clique control*—splitting up teams when the project finishes. As noted earlier in this book, some teams find that the project they're working on is intrinsically boring, and the users to whom they deliver their software are ungrateful louts; so, the satisfaction to be derived from the project comes from the pleasure of working with a certain group of people. Indeed, the satisfaction may be so great that the team members look forward to the prospect of continuing to work together on future projects. But ironically, the team spirit that made the team succeed is often regarded as a political threat to management; hence, the common practice of breaking the team apart upon the completion of the project. This in turn is such a demoralizing prospect that the team disintegrates even before the project deadline.

A final point about team jelling: even when it happens, it doesn't happen on the first day of the project. As Robert Binder [11] observes, a typical team goes through a four-stage evolutionary process, which also applies to the vision-building process of developing a shared understanding of the application problem and general structure of the solution:

- *Forming:* team members define goals, roles, and team direction.
- *Storming:* the team sets rules and decision-making processes, and often renegotiates (argues) over team roles and responsibilities.
- *Norming:* procedures, standards, and criteria are agreed upon.
- *Performing:* the team begins to function as a system.

In the ideal case, a project team may have gone through most of the "forming" and "storming" stages before the project even begins—because the team members have worked together on previous projects. However, every project is different, and every project team usually includes one or two new people, which is bound to cause a certain amount of forming and storming. But, whether the overall process takes a day, or a week, or a month, it must occur; if at all possible, the project manager will try to get the team members assigned to the project well before the official "kick-off" date of the project, in order to be at the "performing" stage when the project officially begins.

It's also important to remember that even when a team has jelled, it can fall apart because of the pressure of the death march project. In an e-mail note to me, Dale Emery [12] recommended that the project manager keep a watchful eye on the team dynamics:

> Pay attention to the relationships within the team, and put some effort into maintaining people's ability to work together over time. A death march project creates tremendous pressure that can amplify small disturbances into major conflicts. Periodic check-ins to "take the temperature" of the group can help you and the team deal with relationship and communication problems while they are still small.

In the worst case, though, the team might never get past the first two stages; or to put it another way, the team may commit teamicide because of the various problems listed earlier. And, by the time the project manager (or some level of management above the project manager) notices that teamicide has occurred, it's probably too late to form a new team. C'est la vie.

4.5 WORKPLACE CONDITIONS FOR DEATH MARCH PROJECTS

The issue of decent offices—versus Dilbert-style cubicles—has been debated for so many years in the software development field that it seems pointless to bring it up again. Tom DeMarco and Tim Lister, whose work has already been cited numerous times in this chapter, have discussed the benefits of decent office working conditions at length in their *Peopleware* opus; software developers who say their workplace is acceptably quiet, for example, are one-third more likely to deliver zero-defect work than those who work in noisy office environments with uncontrollable interruptions. And, in a survey of some 600 software developers, DeMarco and Lister were able to make a persuasive argument that those working in reasonable office conditions—with the ability to divert phone calls, silence the phone, close the door, and prevent needless interruptions—were approximately 2.6 times more productive than those working in the usual office environment.

Though DeMarco and Lister published their work in 1987, it doesn't seem to have done much to the workplace conditions for most software developers—*except in software-product companies.* The working conditions at Microsoft, and in most of the software companies throughout Silicon Valley, are civilized indeed; private offices with doors that close, access to kitchens stocked with soda, juice, and other beverages, and a "permanent" phone number that follows the programmer in the event that he or she is reassigned to a different office.

As for the software developers who work in banks, insurance companies, government agencies, manufacturing organizations, and the hundreds of other companies for whom software is still generally regarded as an "overhead" expense, offices tend to be replaced with cubicles, and the ability to concentrate on one's intellectual efforts ranges from poor to non-existent. Stale Muzak wafts through the air, phones ring incessantly, dogs bark, people yell, and there is no way to prevent anyone from the mailroom messenger to the CEO from butting their head into your office to interrupt you. As DeMarco and Lister put it:

> "Police-mentality planners design workplaces the way they would design prisons: optimized for containment at minimal cost. We have unthinkingly yielded to them on the subject of workplace design, yet for most organizations with productivity problems, there is no more fruitful area for improvement than the workplace.
>
> As long as workers are crowded into noisy, sterile, disruptive space, it's not worth improving anything *but* the workplace."

Unfortunately, my complaining about the situation isn't likely to have any more of an effect on the industry than DeMarco and Lister's far more detailed and eloquent discussion. But remember that we're talking about death march projects here—different rules apply, and I believe that the project manager should adopt the philosophical position that *no* rules apply.

If you're a death march project manager with a nearly-impossible deadline, the message that decent office conditions can lead to a 2.6-fold improvement in productivity should be enough to motivate you to break *lots* of rules. Whatever you accomplish probably won't be permanent; in fact, as soon as the project is over, the furniture police will swoop in and reassign everyone to the same miserable cubicles occupied by the rest of the staff. But, if the death march project only lasts six months, and if you're clever, you might be able to provide decent working conditions without the furniture police even figuring out what's going on.

Here are some possibilities:

- *Frontal attack*—if you have a project champion and/or project owner desperate to get the project finished, explain to him or her just how important it is to put your project team into an effective environment. If the project champion is a high-level manager, it should be relatively easy to arrange a temporary transfer of the project team.

- *The "skunk works" mystique*—most senior managers have heard of the notion of a "skunk works"; thus, rather than asking to locate your project team in the executive suite, where each office has its own private bathroom, ask for permission to relocate the team to an abandoned warehouse.

- *Squatter's rights*—commandeer empty office space that has been sitting unoccupied while the furniture police try to figure out how many hundreds of people they can cram into it. Possession is 90 percent of the battle; while the bureaucracy complains, debates, and sends angry memos back and forth, you might even be able to finish your project and disappear back into the anonymous cubicles again.

- *Telecommute*—tell everyone to work at home, and arrange to have your weekly status meetings at the local McDonald's (at 9AM, when the place is likely to be empty). It may take weeks for anyone to notice that the project team has disappeared. As an additional diversion, you can put scarecrow-style dummies at the desks normally occupied by the project team; management will have a hard time distinguishing them from the other zombies in the office.

- *Switch to the graveyard shift*—this is more extreme, but can be effective if most of the project work can be carried out without interacting with the user community. It's unpleasant asking everyone to change their work schedule to the midnight-to-eight shift, but it's virtually guaranteed to eliminate normal interruptions. A strategy like this is sure to evoke the wrath of bureaucrats throughout the organization, but the wonderful thing is that the bureaucrats aren't in the office in the middle of the night! They'll send angry memos and e-mail messages; but, the best strategy is to ignore them and pretend that you never received them. If that doesn't work, then simply refuse to change your schedule; unless they turn off the lights or change the locks on the office door, there's not much they can do within the duration of a typical death march project.

- *Barricades and buffers*—if your team is in a typical "open office" environment and the strategies discussed above aren't feasible, then do whatever you can to ensure that the project team members are located in contiguous cubicles. Then, take whatever further steps are necessary to barricade that set of cubicles from access by the rest of the office herd. Disable the intercom and loudspeaker that blares noise from the ceiling (and be prepared to do so weekly, as the janitorial service will probably do its best to repair it). Unplug the phones, or as DeMarco/Lister recommend, stuff cotton into the ringer portion of the hand-set. If you can take over an entire floor, or a whole building, so much the better. Erect a pirate flag atop the building, as Steve Jobs did with the Macintosh project team at Apple. Install a guard to shoo away unwanted visitors.

Some of these actions will provoke a more violent response from the corporate bureaucracy than others; the team and its manager will have to decide which strategy is most effective. But, I want to emphasize that I'm serious about *all* of these strategies, despite the obvious fact that they violate the "rules" that one finds in almost every large company. Confronting the bureaucracy in this fashion is not for the timid; but, by the same token, death march projects are not for the timid. If the death march project manager isn't willing to stand up and fight for decent working conditions, then why should the project team be willing to make extraordinary sacrifices on behalf of the organization and project manager [13]? [14]

4.6 SUMMARY

Talented people, cohesive teams, and decent working conditions are not enough to guarantee success in a death march project. The absence of these elements, however, is almost enough to guarantee the project's failure. As we'll see in the next two chapters, good software *processes* and good technology are also important ingredients for success; but, the most important ingredient of all is the people. As Ronald Reagan put it:

> Surround yourself with the best people you can find, delegate authority, and don't interfere.
>
> Ronald Reagan, from *Reagan's Reign of Error*,
> "Mission Impossible" (ed. Mark Green
> and Gail MacColl, 1987).

Notes

1. Ed,
   > 1. How crucial is it for the death march project manager to have
   > the freedom to choose his/her project team members?

   It's another aspect of death march projects that the PM usually has no (or not enough) choice in the people. Having said that, it would be a dream project indeed if you had all the people you wanted - there just aren't enough good people to go around.

   >should the project manager resign on the spot?

   You're assuming that he knows who these people are when he gets them. I've usually had them assigned to me before I know how good/bad they are.

   There is a counter-measure to this, which I have used successfully. Death Marches often end up in the desperate situation where senior management will throw money at you - "You want another twenty people?". And I always accept. I put the bozos onto manning the coffee machine, changing fuses, and other essential work, while I hang on to the better ones. (Randomly, you will get a few good ones). Then you can assist the bozos to resign and keep pressing for more and more people to replace them. In one case, I cut to 20% of the original staffing level, and still maintained work output - but the quality of that output was excellent. That's no surprise to anybody, but it's by constantly demanding more resources and losing them that you can achieve it.

   > 2. How should the project manager handle the issue of rewards?

   The first priority is to take pressure off your staff, so the first

recipient of the rewards should be to the partner and family of
said staff - it's all very well in career/money terms, but it's
the family who have to make the sacrifices. Bouquets of flowers
are a start. Support the whole family - they're the ones doing it.
> 3. What about overtime?
In a death march, it's unavoidable, as you suggest. But part of
scheduling deliveries is to ensure that the overtime comes in
bursts and is then allowed to diminish - you can't keep people
working at 90% and over for very long. I've never been in an
organisation which paid overtime, and I really don't like it—it
smacks of rewarding those who aren't doing well enough. Better to
reward those still standing at the end with bonuses - and that's
counted in months' salaries, not a pie and a pint at the local pub.
> what are the most important things for the manager to do in a
> death march project, vis-a-vis peopleware and teamwork?
Be there. Listen. Represent their views back to senior management,
and ensure that the trivia is dealt with quickly and efficiently.
Get the coffee, if that's all he can effectively do. Contribute.
> what are the most important things they should do for themselves,
 > and for their fellow team-mates, during the project?
The same. Help each other, so that the work gets done in the
quickest possible time. You might even get home early.
I note that I'm worrying a lot about married folk, but that's
because the spouses are often ignored in death marches, and I've
seen many a marriage (including my own) go west because of a death
march. It needn't be so, if managed well. Single folk have more
freedom to choose, and less reason to feel trapped.
--Doug

2. Tom DeMarco and Tim Lister, *Peopleware* (Dorset House Publishing, 1987).

3. See Note 1.

4. Frederick Herzberg, "One More Time: How Do You Motivate Employees?" *Harvard Business Review,* September-October 1987.

5. See Note 1.

6. This wonderful strategy was suggested by *Peopleware* guru Larry Constantine at a software conference in Melbourne, sponsored by the Australian Computer Society in 1995.

7. Ed,
>> 2. How should the project manager handle the issue of rewards?
<<

>> 3. What about overtime? While rational people might argue that overtime is not a good idea for "normal" projects, it's pretty hard to avoid in a death march project. How much should be expected? << How much can be afforded? Unless stock options for the company are distributed to team members as generously to senior management, there are no forms of compensation for a death march that would qualify as a reward (I'm using reward as a term with a positive tone). While the PM rarely has this control over compensation, what really should be done is immediate compensated overtime in the next paycheck. This gives something back to the people sacrificing the most for the project, and punishes (through the budget) the people who need to learn the real cost of a project (senior mgmt, etc). If you're going to do a death march, it's best to get paid by the mile.
- Dave

8. See note 1.

9. John Boddie, *Crunch Mode* (Prentice-Hall/Yourdon Press, 1987), page 124.

10. Rob Thomsett, "Effective Project Teams: A Dilemma, a Model, a Solution," *American Programmer*, July–August 1990.

11. Binder's article on team evolution.

12. Ed,

>> 1. How crucial is it for the death march project manager to have the freedom to choose his/her project team members? No one doubts that it's important, but _how_ important? If senior management says, "Sorry, but the only available people for this project are Neurotic Ned, Moron Mary, and Zombie Zack", should the project manager resign on the spot? << Freedom to choose project team members is about as crucial as your freedom to decide any other parameter of the project. Even if you can't choose the schedule, you can still be honest about how that schedule will affect other parameters. Even if you can choose the project team members, you can still be honest about how their capabilities will affect other parameters.

>> 4. Aside from the issue of managing overtime, what are the most important things for the manager to do in a death march project, vis-a-vis peopleware and teamwork? << Always remember that the people working for you on the project are exactly as important as you and your manager, and exactly as important as the project's customers. If you allow this balance to tilt, and start treating the people on the team as if their needs

are not important to you, they'll very quickly get the hint. Then, guess what happens to the commitment you wrote about earlier. Pay attention to the relationships within the team, and put some effort into maintaining people's ability to work together over time. A death march project creates tremendous pressure that can amplify small disturbances into major conflicts. Periodic check-ins to "take the temperature" of the group can help you and the team deal with relationship and communication problems while they are still small.

>> 5. Same question from the perspective of the team members: what are the most important things they should do for themselves, and for their fellow team-mates, during the project? <<

Stay in touch with what you are giving up and what you are gaining by working on the project. Check now and then to make sure the balance is in your favor. If it isn't, do something to get it back in your favor. The key is to stay aware of what you need and what you're willing to do to get it.

Remember that you are here by choice. Work on improving your alternatives to continuing on the death march project. It is marvelous what having choices can do for your attitude.

--Dale

13. On the other hand, one of the problems of tactics that is guaranteed to annoy the bureaucracy is that key people outside the team may become reluctant to help you. As Paul Neuhardt explained in a recent e-mail message to me:

> When it became obvious that we were lost in the desert, I kept things going for a time with the old "We'll get things going again soon" speech. Before long, any moron could see this project wasn't going anywhere, so I looked for a new approach. I tried "Hey, let's do it our way and to heck with management." This worked for awhile, but some of the key people we needed outside of the team were so scared of management that they wouldn't help us until we got the green light from the executive suite. Next was, "There's a management shakeup in the works. If we outlive the current managers, we can get back on track." Yeah, right. The faces changed but the song remained the same.

14. Ed,

I will confess here and publicly: I was a failure as a death march manager. At least, I think I was. The reason I say that is that eventually I lost the ability to keep my team motivated.

My experiences as manager of death marches are both what I described earlier as "Lost Patrol" projects. They might not have

been death marches if we ever had a fixed target to shoot for, but
with the goal changing daily we thrashed along forever with
expectations from senior management high and our ability to succeed
becoming increasingly low. I had built a team of people who
genuinely believed in the project. They wanted to learn new
technologies, broaden themselves and improve the state of the
systems at the company. And, while bonuses for completing a project
weren't going to be handed out, there were promotions, raises and
prestige to be had, all of which motivated my team.

When it became obvious that we were lost in the desert, I kept
things going for a time with the old "We'll get things going again
soon" speech. Before long, any moron could see this project wasn't
going anywhere, so I looked for a new approach. I tried "Hey, let's
do it our way and to heck with management." This worked for awhile,
but some of the key people we needed outside of the team were so
scared of management that they wouldn't help us until we got the
green light from the executive suite. Next was, "There's a
management shakeup in the works. If we outlive the current
managers, we can get back on track." Yeah, right. The faces changed
but the song remained the same.

By this time I was probably the most disgruntled person on the
project. I had not only been sent into the desert to die, but I
had convinced several people I liked and respected to come with
me. I was not only mad, I was guilty. Needless to say, when all
you want to do is throw one rip-snorter of tantrum ending in the
words "Take this job and shove it" it is pretty close to impossible
to motivate people to keep marching. I know I couldn't find what
it took inside of me. I found another job, apologized to the team
for taking them into Hell with me, and left. In this at least I
managed to lead by example. Of the 10 people on my team one year
ago, only one still works for that company.

Not that this is what you asked for, but I feel better for having
gotten to say it. And no, I'm not paying you $150/hr (or whatever
it is that shrinks get these days). I will, however, buy you a
drink next time you are in Boston. Look me up.
--Paul

Additional References

Rich Cohen and Warren Keuffel, "Pull Together," *Software Magazine*, August 1991.

Larry Constantine, *Constantine on Peopleware* (Englewood Cliffs, NJ: Prentice Hall, 1995). ISBN: 0-13-331976-8.

Daniel J. Couger and Robert A. Zawacki, *Motivating and Managing Computer Personnel* (New York: John Wiley & Sons, 1980). ISBN: 0-471084-85-9.

B. Curtis, W.E. Hefley, and S. Miller, *People Capability Maturity Model*, Draft version 0.3 (Pittsburgh, PA: Software Engineering Institute, April 1995).

Tom DeMarco and Timothy Lister, "Programmer Productivity and the Effects of the Workplace," *Proceedings of the 8th ICSE* (Washington, DC: IEEE Press, 1985).

Richard J. Hackman (ed.), *Groups That Work (and Those That Don't): Creating Conditions for Effective Teamwork* (San Francisco, CA: Jossey-Bass, 1990). ISBN: 1-555421-87-3.

Watts Humphrey, *Managing for Innovation: Leading Technical People* (New York: McGraw-Hill, 1987). ISBN: 0-135503-02-07.

Magid Igbaria and Jeffrey H. Greenhaus, "Determinants of MIS Employees' Turnover Intentions," *Communications of the ACM*, February 1992.

J.R. Katzenbach and D.K. Smith, *The Wisdom of Teams* (Boston, MA: Harvard University Press, 1993). ISBN: 0-8754843067-0.

Guy Kawasaki, *The Macintosh Way: The Art of Guerrilla Management* (Glenview, IL: Scott Foresman and Company, 1989). ISBN 0-06-097338-2.

J. P. Klubnik, *Rewarding and Recognizing Employees* (Chicago, IL: Irwin Publishers, 1995).

Otto Kroeger and Janet M. Thuesen, *Type Talk: The 16 Personalities That Determine How We Live, Love, and Work* (New York: Bantam Doubleday, 1988). ISBN: 0-440-50704-9.

Susan A. Mohrman, Susan G. Cohen, and Allan M. Mohrman, Jr., *Designing Team-Based Organizations* (San Francisco, CA: Jossey-Bass, 1995).

Peter Senge, *The Fifth Discipline: The Art and Practice of the Learning Organization* (New York: Doubleday, 1990). ISBN: 0-385260-94-6.

S.B. Sheppard, B. Curtis, P. Milliman, and T. Love, "Modern Coding Practices and Programmer Performance," *IEEE Computer*, December 1979.

Paul Strassmann, "Internet: A Way for Outsourcing Infomercenaries?" *American Programmer*, August 1995.

Auren Uris, *88 Mistakes Interviewers Make and How to Avoid Them* (New York: American Management Association, 1988).

J.D. Valett and F.E. McGarry, "A Summary of Software Measurement Experiences in the Software Engineering Laboratory," *Journal of Systems and Software*, Vol. 9, No. 2, 1989, pp. 137–148.

Susan Webber, "Performance Management: A New Approach to Software Engineering Management," *American Programmer*, July–August 1990.

Gerald M. Weinberg, *The Psychology of Computer Programming* (New York: Van Nostrand Reinhold, 1971). ISBN: 0-442-29264-3.

Gerald M. Weinberg, *Understanding the Professional Programmer* (New York: Dorset House, 1988). ISBN: 0-932633-09-9.

Mike West, "Empowerment: Five Meditations on the Soul of Software Development," *American Programmer*, July–August 1990.

Ken Whitaker, *Managing Software Maniacs* (New York: John Wiley & Sons, 1994). ISBN: 0-471-00997-0.

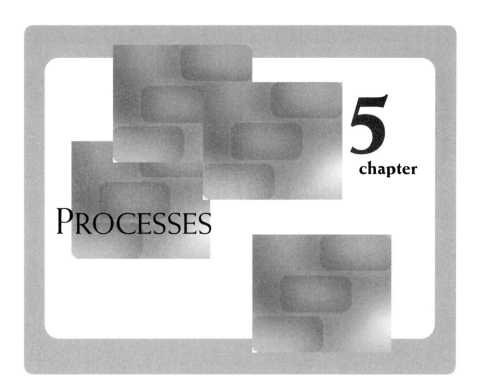

5 chapter

PROCESSES

No delusion is greater than the notion that method and industry can make up for lack of mother-wit, either in science or in practical life.

Thomas Henry Huxley

"On the Advisableness of Improving Natural Knowledge"
(1866; reprinted in Collected Essays,
vol. 1, 1893)

There is a point at which methods devour themselves.

Frantz Fanon, *Black Skins, White Masks,*
Introduction (1952; translated 1967)

If you remember only one word from this chapter—or for that matter, the entire book you are now reading—it should be *triage*. You might have assumed, from the title of this chapter, that I would be concentrating on familiar methodologies like structured analysis, or formal process disciplines like the SEI Capability Maturity Model (CMM), or various prototyping approaches generically referred to as RAD (for "Rapid Application Development"). These are all important and relevant ideas, but the most important idea of all is this: *You don't have enough time in a death march project to do everything the users are asking for.* If you build your processes and methods around that sobering fact, you have a chance of succeeding; if you begin the project with the notion that coding can't commence until all the structured analysis data flow diagrams have been approved by the user, you'll definitely fail.

This doesn't mean that we should ignore all of the other process-related ideas and strategies (I'll cover them later in this chapter); but as you'll see, my general opinion is that they should be introduced as part of a *strategic* corporate decision, rather than foisted upon a death-project team as a desperate tactical ploy to avoid what would otherwise be a failure. And the concept of triage applies here, too—if pressed, a death march project team will abandon the methods it feels is unhelpful or unessential (like detailed mini-specs in a structured analysis model), and devote its resources to whatever it feels is most helpful. Similarly, a project manager who has only a few moments to read this chapter should read the most important information, and skip the rest if necessary; I've organized the discussion in this chapter with that in mind.

5.1 THE CONCEPT OF "TRIAGE"

The word "triage" comes from the Old French *trier*, which means "to sort." The *American Heritage Dictionary* (3rd edition) defines it as follows:

> **tri·age** (trê-äzh´, trê´äzh´y) noun
>
> 1.   A process for sorting injured people into groups based on their need for or likely benefit from immediate medical treatment. Triage is used on the battlefield, at disaster sites, and in hospital emergency rooms when limited medical resources must be allocated.
>
> 2.   A system used to allocate a scarce commodity, such as food, only to those capable of deriving the greatest benefit from it.

Most of us are familiar with the medical connotation of triage, but the second dictionary definition is more relevant for our discussion of death march projects: allocating a scarce commodity (the scarcest of which is usually *time*) in such a way as to derive the greatest benefit from it. Or, as Stephen Covey puts it in *First Things First* [1], "the main thing is to make sure that the main thing *is* the main thing." (Indeed, the project is likely to achieve far more benefit by giving every staff member a copy of Covey's excellent book than a ponderous tome on software engineering methodologies!)

Most prototyping and RAD approaches are compatible with triage, and a few even mention the concept explicitly. But, the emphasis in most RAD approaches is simply to get something—anything!—working quickly, so that it can be demonstrated to the user in order to (a) demonstrate that tangible progress has been made, and (b) solicit feedback on the functionality of the system and (mostly) on the user interface. That's all very useful, but if the project team has devoted its resources to building initial prototypes with "sexy" but nonetheless non-essential features, the team *and* the user are wasting their time.

The reason for this is because of the subtle, but insidious, assumption made by most software engineering methodologies—whether they are based on the classic "waterfall" life cycle, or the more recent "spiral" and prototyping methodologies. The assumption is that, "somehow, we'll get it *all* done by the time the deadline arrives." Perhaps this is because many of us grew up in households where we were told by our parents that we had to finish *everything* on our plates before we could leave the dinner table; in any case, the unspoken motto of many project teams is, "we will leave no requirement unfulfilled."

A noble motto indeed, but almost always unachievable in a death march project. As I mentioned in Chapter 1, most death march projects have "official" requirements that exceed the team's resources—specifically, people resources and time resources—by 50-100 percent. The response by the naive death march project team is to hope that by working double overtime, the deficit can somehow be overcome; the response by the cynical suicide mission team is to assume that the project will end up 50-100 percent behind schedule, just like every other project. But, even the cynical team is usually wrong, for they still assume that sooner or later (usually *much* later!) they'll eventually implement all of the functionality requested by the user.

The key point about death march projects is that not only will some requirements remain unfulfilled when the official deadline arrives, but some of them *will never be implemented*. Assuming that the familiar "80-20" rule holds true, the project team might be able to deliver 80 percent of the "benefit" of the system by implementing 20 percent of the requirements—*if* they implement the right 20 percent. And, since the user is often desperate to put the system into operation far earlier than the project team thinks reasonable, the user might take that 20 percent, begin using it, and never bother asking for the remaining 80 percent of the system's functionality.

This is extreme and simplistic, of course, but in virtually all of the death march projects that I've been involved with, it made enormous good sense to separate the system requirements, triage-style, into "must-do," "should-do," and "could-do" categories. The meaning of these three terms is obvious, and the fact that there are only three prevents any irrelevant squabbles as to whether a specific requirement should be categorized as a "priority-6" or "priority-7" requirement. Having performed such a triage, the obvious project strategy is to focus on the "must-do" requirements first; if there is time left over, then focus on the "should-do" requirements; and, if a miracle occurs, then work on the "could-do" requirements.

Failure to follow such a strategy *from the beginning of the project* usually leads to an ugly crisis toward the end of the project; in addition to the nasty politics, it also produces what my colleague Dean Leffingwell at Requisite, Inc. refers to as "wasted inventory." To understand why, consider the typical project time-line shown in Figure 5.1:

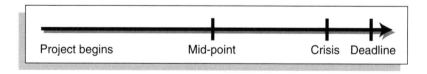

FIGURE 5.1 A PROJECT TIME-LINE

When the project begins, nobody is willing to admit that the schedule is unrealistic—least of all the user and senior management! The project manager and team members may have a bad feeling in the pit of their stomach that they've gotten into a suicide mission, but if they're optimistic, they may believe that it will be a mission impossible-style project where a miracle saves them later on. The key point here is that the deadline is far enough away—typically six months or a year—that nobody has to face up to the reality that the objectives are impossible.

Indeed, the political pressures and the team's naiveté may even prevent a reassessment midway through the project. Ironically, the problem is often compounded if the project team has been following some form of RAD/prototyping approach, for they've probably demonstrated one or more prototype versions of the system to the user, which can prolong the illusion that everything will be done on time. But by now, the project team is probably beginning to realize that they're in over their heads; and if it's the manager's first death march project, he or she often has the naive belief that senior management and the user will eventually come to their senses.

Alas, things don't usually work out that way. An "ugly crisis" finally occurs when the user and/or senior management finally must face the undeniable reality that despite the demands and despite the sincere promises from the project manager, the system is not going to be delivered on time. This often occurs a month before the deadline, sometimes a week before, and sometimes the day *after* the official deadline! Depending on how the political battles have been proceeding up to this point, and depending on how exhausted and frustrated the project manager has become, there are several possible outcomes. But, what often happens is that senior management concludes that the entire problem is the fault of the project manager; that hapless individual is summarily fired (if he hasn't quit already!), and a new project manager is brought in with blunt instructions to "clean this mess up, and get the system delivered."

The replacement manager may be a battle-scarred veteran from within the organization, or perhaps a consultant from the outside. And sometimes, the new manager *does* find that his predecessor made a number of basic management mistakes (e.g., no schedule at all, or no work breakdown schedule); sometimes, the new manager's 20-20 hindsight concludes that the original manager was basically doing the right things, but couldn't avoid becoming the sacrificial scapegoat when senior management finally had to accept the fact that their original demands were impossible to achieve.

But whatever the assessment, one thing is almost certain: The replacement project manager must address the fact that the complete set of project requirements cannot be finished in time for the original deadline—if that weren't the case, the original project manager probably wouldn't have been fired in the first place. So, what does the replacement manager do? The two most obvious options [2] are:

- Renegotiate the deadline
- Renegotiate the system requirements

The first option might be acceptable, but it's unlikely in a death march project. After all, the reason the users were asking for an unreasonable schedule in the first place is that they desperately need the system to cope with some business demand. And, since the negotiation being carried out by the replacement project manager is taking place at a point in time relatively close to the original deadline, there's a good chance that the user community has already begun making plans of its own to put the new system into operation. The last thing they want to hear is that it's going to be delayed another 6-12 months.

Thus, the most common—and successful—negotiating ploy involves a triage of the original requirements. Note that the replacement project manager is negotiating from a position of strength—it's not his or her fault that the project is in such a mess, and there's an unspoken awareness that management and the users were pretty stupid to have gotten themselves into this situation in the first place. The new project manager may even base his or her acceptance of the assignment on a successful outcome of the negotiations—e.g., with a statement like, "If you want me to take over this disastrous project, then you're going to have to accept the fact that we can only deliver a small percentage of the original functionality in time for your deadline. That's the situation; take it or leave it."

So far, all of this is fairly straightforward—even though it's discouraging, as a consultant, to see it happening over and over again. But, this is where Requisite Inc.'s Dean Leffingwell asks the question, "What about the inventory?" That is, what about all of the work-in-progress created by the project team *before* the "ugly crisis" occurred and the new project manager took over? Chances are that the project team has written a lot of code, and maybe some test cases; they might even have some documentation, and design models, and structured analysis models. What happens to all of that "inventory" of partially completed work? The sobering answer: *most of it gets thrown away.*

This might seem like an unnecessarily pessimistic statement. After all, why not simply put all of that partly-finished work aside, and return to it later on? In the best of all worlds, this is exactly what happens; but, it presumes the existence of a good set of tools and processes for version control, configuration management, source code control, etc.—all of which may have been abandoned in the heat of battle, when the team was concentrating on producing as much output as possible.

The real reason why all of this partially-completed work ends up being wasted inventory is that *no one will ever have time to come back to it.* Assuming that the project team members (now under the control of a new manager, whom they may or may not respect) is able to deliver the "bare minimum" of critical functionality, they're usually so exhausted that half of them quit. And the users are so disgusted with the project that they never bother asking for the rest of the unfinished functionality; or conversely, they're so satisfied with the minimal functionality that they never bother asking for the rest of the system. Even if they do, and even if the original team is still intact, there's a good chance that so many architectural changes were made in the attempt to deliver a "bare-bones" system that the half-finished pieces of work (which relate to non-critical requirements) can no longer be used.

Note that none of this discussion has anything to do with structured analysis, the SEI-CMM, or any other "textbook" methodologies and software processes. It's just common sense; but it's *critical* common sense in a death march project. For it to work, *all* of the shareholders and stakeholders must agree as to which requirements fall into the "must-do" category, which ones are "should-do," and which ones are "could-do" requirements. Obviously, if the project owner categorically insists that *all* of the requirements are "must-do" items, and that nothing falls into the other two categories, this whole discussion is a waste of time [3]. And, if the various shareholders and stakeholders cannot reach a consensus about the triage items, then the project team will be paralyzed, attempting to do everything for everybody when they lack the resources to do so.

Unfortunately, the "ultimate reality" is that most organizations lack the discipline, experience, or political strength to deal with these issues at the beginning of the project. Nothing that I've described in the preceding paragraphs is "rocket science," and even the most technologically illiterate manager or business user can understand the issues; indeed, they would apply just as well to *any* kind of project that has to cope with limited resources and inadequate time. But even though everyone understands the issues intellectually, the political battles surrounding death march projects makes it almost impossible to reach a consensus on a reasonable triage. It's only when the "ugly crisis" occurs that the various parties finally agree on something that they should have agreed upon when the project began.

The exception to this gloomy prognosis is the organization that has adopted death march projects as a way of life. Obviously, users and senior managers are not stupid, and they usually learn from their experiences— even if it takes three or four disasters for the lessons to sink in. As mentioned above, the original death march project manager is usually a victim of the inability to perform an early triage, but the survivors gradually figure out what it's all about. I'll have more to say about this in Chapter 7.

5.2 THE IMPORTANCE OF REQUIREMENTS MANAGEMENT

The discussion above suggests that death march projects need to focus on a new aspect of the system development life cycle: *requirements*. Why do I say "new"? After all, every project has requirements, and it's not as if software developers are completely unaware of the concept.

Traditional software engineering methodologies—including the various "structured" and "object-oriented" methodologies that several of my colleagues and I have developed over the past 20 years—have concentrated on *modeling* the requirements, usually with graphical techniques such as data flow diagrams or entity-relationship diagrams. What I'm talking about in this chapter is *managing* the requirements during the hectic days of a death march project.

These two concepts—modeling and managing—are not contradictory or incompatible. You can devote time and energy to both of them; if a death march project team finds that it's helpful to draw object-oriented analysis models to form a better understanding of the requirements of their system, I have no objection. My only caveat is that the team should do what *it* thinks important and helpful, not what the Methodology Police think is "proper." [4]

My experience has been that the majority of death march projects do *not* use formal modeling techniques such as SA/SD or OOA/OOD. Sometimes it's because they think these methodologies are too cumbersome and bureaucratic; sometimes it's because they think the CASE tools that support them are too clumsy; and often, it's because they don't see an automated means of translating their analysis models into working code—which, they realize, is the *only* thing the user cares about [5].

Indeed, in the extreme case, the project team won't document any of the user requirements; their defense (which every project manager has heard by now!) is that it takes too long, it is too susceptible to change, and besides, the users don't really know what they want anyway. Thus, the team typically relies on prototyping tools and methods, both to produce the all-important visible evidence of progress throughout the death march schedule, and also to elicit the true requirements of the system.

From the "triage" perspective of Section 5.1, there's one major problem with this: It doesn't give us an organized way to *manage* the requirements. At any moment in time, how can we tell which requirements are "must-do," which ones are "should-do," and which ones are "could-do"? It's interesting to note that the SA/SD and OOA/OOD methodologies don't focus on this either. One could document the prioritization decisions by color-coding the bubbles in a data-flow diagram, but that's not what the diagram was originally intended for. SA/SD and OOA/OOD are intended more for *understanding* and *explaining* the requirements than for managing them in a dynamic fashion.

It's the *dynamic* element of requirements management that usually

causes the difficulties. If we could get all of the shareholders and stakeholders to agree on the triage priorities at the beginning of the project,
and if those priorities never changed throughout the duration of the
project .... well, if you believe *that*, then you probably believe in the tooth
fairy, too. What happens in *real* death march projects is usually a combination of the following dilemmas:

- The shareholders and stakeholders can't agree completely on the
  triage priorities. Of course, if they are in total disagreement, the
  project is paralyzed; but, it's not uncommon to see 80 percent of
  the requirements prioritized, and then the project commences
  while the politicians continue to squabble about the remaining 20
  percent. High-priority requirements sometimes emerge at the last
  moment from this squabbling. This drives the project team nuts,
  but that doesn't prevent it from happening.

- Circumstances change within the team, while the project continues. For example, the project manager arrives in the office one
  morning and discovers that his two best programmers, Matilda and
  Ezekiel, have decided to form a reggae band, and have just left for
  Nashville to seek a recording contract. These things aren't supposed to happen, but they do. The manager's first three questions
  are, "What 'must-do' requirements were those two scoundrels
  working on, what was the status of those requirements, and to
  whom can I reassign them?"

- Circumstances change *outside* the project team. Budgets are
  expanded or reduced, depending on the company's financial for-
  tunes. Deadlines are moved up or moved back (though hardly ever
  back!) as the marketing department becomes aware of changes in
  the competitive situation of the marketplace. Government regulations change, technology changes (not always for the better!), suppliers come and go, etc., etc. Each of these external events is likely
  to have some impact on the triage decisions.

- There is often a "moment of truth" when the users, senior management, and project team members have to admit that they won't finish the system in time. Of course, if they have done a good job of
  triage prioritization at the beginning of the project, this crisis might

not occur at all. But, what if the team has to confess that it can't even finish all of the "must-do" requirements in time for the deadline? As noted earlier, the original project manager is usually beheaded and a replacement is brought in; and, if the new manager can extend the deadline, then the triage decisions may not have to be changed. But, it's also common at this point to see a hard-nosed reevaluation of those early triage decisions. With the deadline looming only a few weeks away, the users might be forced to admit that some requirements they had earlier described as *absolutely* essential are not so essential after all.

I could continue with these scenarios, but you get the point: managing the priority of requirements is a critical part of the "process" of death march projects. Now, this would be a straightforward activity if a death march project only had a dozen requirements; we could scribble them on a paper napkin and simply review them whenever necessary. But, most projects have hundreds of requirements, and many have thousands; the Boeing 777 aircraft (which could be regarded as a bunch of software with wings) is rumored to have had 300,000 requirements. Not only that, the requirements usually can't be treated as independent, stand-alone items; some requirements are dependent on other requirements, and some requirements spawn (or are further described by) sub-requirements.

This implies the need for methods, processes, and tools for representing the relationships between requirements, and for managing large quantities of relationships. And in this area, familiar techniques such as structured analysis and object-oriented analysis *do* help; unfortunately, those techniques have traditionally ignored the *attributes* of a requirement, such as priority, cost, risk, schedule, owner, and the developer to whom it has been assigned. As a result, the project teams that have been aware of the need for managing their requirements have used home-grown tools based on spreadsheets, word processors, or jury-rigged 4GL databases to provide some degree of automation support.

Fortunately, a new breed of software tools is emerging to provide a more comprehensive and sophisticated degree of support. Some of the tools now available are: Requisite (from Requisite, Inc.), DOORS (from Zycad Corp.), and RTM (from Marconi Systems). Since this chapter is concerned with processes rather than tools, I won't go into the details of these three products; but since tools *affect* processes, it's important that you know they exist [6].

There is one aspect of the process-tool combination that deserves special mention here. As noted earlier, many death march project teams abandon formal SA/SD or OOA/OOD methodologies because they feel they are too bureaucratic and time-consuming. Interestingly, the share-holders and stake-holders feel the same way. Given their choice, they would prefer not to be forced to learn how to read data flow diagrams; in-deed, the higher-level echelons of managers and end users will complain that they don't understand all of those "technical" diagrams. They also have little patience for wading through hundreds of pages of diagrams and meticulous details about data element definitions or process specifi-cations. With enough time and patience, the project team can overcome the resistance and persuade the end users that the elaborate models are useful indeed—but in death march projects, there is very little time and very little patience.

What the users *can* understand is their own native language—e.g., English for most North American projects. And, what most users *are* will-ing to read is a terse document of 10-20 pages that summarizes the re-quirements for the system. The requirements may be referred to as "features" in such a document, and the overall document may be known as a "Product Requirements Document" (PRD) or "high-level specifica-tion" or some other convenient phrase. But, the key point is that it's En-glish, it's terse, and it's to the point. It shouldn't contain a lot of marketing "fluff," and it shouldn't have obscure terminology or notation that makes key users stop and ask, "What on earth does *this* mean?" Ide-ally, each paragraph, or even each individual sentence, should be directly related to a requirement that both users and project team members can use as a starting point for their subsequent work.

The interesting thing about this is that we already have a familiar tool for creating such requirements documents; it's called a word processor. Indeed, the initial version of such a document often emerges from the us-er's world—e.g., in the form of a memo from the Marketing VP to the CEO about the need for a sexy new Widget product with features X, Y, and Z to compete against the Whizbang product from Blatzco, Inc.—

even before the IS/IT department hears about it. At this early stage, the users view the word processor as *their* tool, and they view the marketing memo as *their* document; as a result, they're usually far more willing to participate in subsequent discussions about triage prioritization if the same tools and documents can continue to be used. Thus, we're beginning to see a shift towards *document-centric* requirements management, where the tools used by the IS/IT specialists (e.g., Requisite, DOORS, or RTM) are tightly integrated with the word processing tools and documents that the users understand [7].

One last point about all of this: It's essential that *all* of the shareholders and stakeholders be involved in the process of creating the initial requirements document and carrying out the triage prioritization. This is true for all projects, of course, but the time-pressure and political squabbles associated with death march projects often tempts the project manager into thinking, "Well, we'll just forge ahead without that idiot Melvin in Marketing; all he'll do is disagree with everything, anyway..." The problem is that Melvin often turns out to have some significant political clout, and if he feels he's being ignored (and that the project manager thinks he's an idiot!), he'll probably find a way to sabotage the project.

In theory, everyone understands and agrees with this point—but in practice, it's amazing to see how many requirements sneak into death march projects. Additional requirements, modifications to existing requirements, and not-so-subtle suggestions to ignore certain requirements—all of these will come in "over the transom" to the project team, in the form of conversations, e-mail messages, and one-on-one meetings with the project manager. Many of these suggestions will be prefaced by such smooth words as, "Sorry I didn't think about bringing this up in our meeting last week, but..." or "I wish we had time to run this new requirement by the formal steering group, but..."

Whether the project manager has a formal steering group—i.e., a group that represents the shareholders and stakeholders, and that reviews the progress of the project and makes the definitive decisions about triage priorities—is something I won't comment on; this depends on each organization's style of managing and running projects. But what *is* essential, for the survival of the death march project, is that the modifications to the original requirements "baseline" be documented and be made publicly visible for all of the shareholders and stakeholders to see. If the VP of Finance wants to slip a new high-priority requirement into the project, that's fine; but the project manager should ensure that the VP of Marketing and the CEO can see that it's there.

5.3 SEI, ISO-9000, AND FORMAL VS. INFORMAL PROCESSES

Some project managers might read the preceding section of this chapter and complain, "Wow! That sounds *much* more formal than anything we've ever done!" Having encountered such a reaction in some consulting engagements, I'm often stymied. On the one hand, I believe that the documentation, prioritization, and management of requirements is essential (regardless of what tools or techniques are used to accomplish the task); on the other hand, I worry that if an entirely new, alien process is introduced into a project team that already has more than it can handle, the new concept—e.g., requirements management—may turn out to be the straw that breaks the camel's back.

Indeed, I don't have a good answer for this dilemma, other than hoping that perhaps the project team will be able to manage *one* new idea among their collection of tools and processes. But, I worry even more when I see teams embarking upon a death march project with the decision (or more commonly, the edict foisted upon them by the Methodology Police) that they *must* embrace a formal process approach such as the SEI-CMM or ISO-9000. Formal processes are great if you know what you're doing, and if you've used the processes before. But, the reality is that such formal processes typically *haven't* been used at all in the organization; the death march project is the pilot project for structured analysis or ISO-9000.

What insanity! It really *is* the straw that breaks the camel's back; after all, the typical death march project is trying to do something that's never been done before, and (despite my warnings in Chapter 4) the team often consists of people who have never worked together before. As if that wasn't enough, now they have to learn how to use an unfamiliar methodology or process, one which they're not sure they believe in the first place, and one which they're convinced will slow them down. Why is it that the Methodology Police are so surprised to see resistance in circumstances like these? Consultant Doug Scott gave me an example of this situation in a recent e-mail message [8]:

> On one project I know, they needed a diagrammer for the ERDs, so they bought Excelerator. Having found that it supported SSADM (which must be the methodologist's methodology) they adopted it without any training or induction for the staff. Then they found that the pace of the project slowed significantly (in fact, it nearly halted) while everyone was busy reading manuals and learning software tools and deciding what they should do next (and re-doing what they had done earlier in the "wrong" sequence). For death march watchers, an almost ideal scenario. Oh, and the project manager was sacked half way through the project, but that's normal.

And as Paul Maskens argued in another e-mail message [9]:

> A death march project is not the time for staff to learn a new (or their first) methodology. OTOH it would contribute greatly to the chances of project death if they *did* learn a new methodology at the same time.

To succeed, the death march project team needs to agree on which processes will be formalized—perhaps source code control and change management, and (hopefully) requirements management—and which processes will be carried out on a completely ad hoc basis (e.g., user-interface design). There's no point mandating a particular software process if it's not going to be followed. The Methodology Police is wasting its time if it tries to do so, and it will cause the project team to waste *its* time, which is far more valuable (in many cases, the Methodology Police members have nothing useful to do anyway, other than to run around the IS/IT department harassing hapless project teams!).

This means that the death march project manager must impose the processes that he or she feels essential, in a dictatorial fashion—e.g., "Anyone who modifies our source code without going through the change management process will be fired summarily!" Or, the project team must *sincerely* agree to adopt the process, because they believe that it will be cost-effective. This is more likely to occur if the project team has worked together before, so that they share a common experience with various software development processes; it's less likely to occur if one team member stands up and says, "I deeply believe that structured analysis is critical to the success of our project," when the other team members have no idea what he or she is talking about. Another corollary of this principle: It's usually a disaster to introduce a new, unfamiliar process into a death march project, even if the team collectively believes that it will help. The learning curve, and the inevitable confusion and bickering over the details of the process, will usually outweigh its benefits.

This means that such formal approaches as SEI-CMM, ISO-9000, or the introduction of new analysis/design methodologies should be done somewhere outside the death march project. The sensible thing to do is to introduce these processes as part of a long-term corporate strategy, to experiment first with a pilot project (which should *not* be a death march project), and then support it with appropriate training. As Sharon Marsh Roberts put it in a recent e-mail message [10] to me:

> Cowpokes don't need the manure to be cleaned from the pasture. Programmers don't need to have the "methodology" gurus clean up the deliverables.
>
> But if someone wants to have a formal software process, then the folks doing the programming should be protected from that extra effort.

If all of these things have been done, and if all the other development projects are already operating at level-3 on the SEI-CMM scale, *then* it becomes interesting to ask whether such processes should also be used on a death march project. As Watts Humphrey once remarked in a conference speech about the SEI-CMM, "If a process can't be used in a crisis, it shouldn't be used at all."

I'm not sure that many would agree with Humphrey's assertion, particularly if the death march project is viewed as a once-in-a-lifetime exception to the norm. If indeed this is the case, then perhaps it does make sense to abandon the formal processes, and let the death march team use whatever *ad hoc* techniques they feel appropriate. But remember my assertion in Chapter 1: Death march projects are becoming the norm, not the exception. If this is the case, then the official corporate processes should be amended, as necessary, to make them suitable for the death march project. Then, and only then, does Humphrey's statement make sense.

In the meantime, if you *do* feel compelled to make a death march project team practice some form of process improvement, my recommendation is to look at Watts Humphrey's PSP, or Personal Software Process. I summarized its characteristics in my *Rise and Resurrection of the American Programmer*. You should also read Humphrey's *A Discipline of Software Engineering* [11]. Fair warning though: It's 789 pages long.

5.4 "GOOD ENOUGH" SOFTWARE

The triage prioritization discussed above can go a long way toward making a death march project "rational" in its behavior. For success, it's not required to implement *all* of the requirements; it's "good enough" if we can implement the "must-do" requirements and a reasonable number of the "should-do" requirements.

But, there's another aspect of software development that causes difficulty in death march projects: the implicit demand for *absolute* quality. This is usually expressed in terms of defects (bugs), but it may also be expressed in terms of portability, platform independence, flexibility, maintainability, and a few dozen other "ilities." It's hard enough to achieve these objectives in normal projects; it's almost impossible to do so in death march projects. Instead, the project team must decide—and if at all possible, get concurrence from the shareholders and stakeholders—what's *good enough*.

The reason that this is so important is that the achievement of absolute "ilities" consumes project resources—especially time. If you want to develop a certifiably bug-free program, complete with a mathematical proof of correctness, it's going to take time. It may also require a higher level of talent than the project team can provide. It's also going to consume some of the energy of one or more people on the project team, which means that those people won't be available to work on other requirements. In short, achieving such "ilities" such as reliability, portability, and maintainability requires a trade-off, and it must be taken into account as part of the triage prioritization discussed above.

Death march project teams must confront this unpleasant reality, because the alternative is usually "perfect" software that isn't finished when the all-important deadline arrives. It's better if the team is aware of the pragmatics of good-enough software at the beginning of the project; but, my experience has been that many traditional software developers accept the notion of good-enough software development only when their backs are against the wall—e.g., when they're facing the "ugly crisis" discussed earlier, a month or two before the deadline.

Up to that point, they'll complain, "How would you like it if we used your 'good-enough' approach for the software in a nuclear reactor or an air traffic control system?" The answer, of course, is that I wouldn't like it at all; and, if someone proposed a death march project for those kinds of high-reliability applications, I would stop flying on airplanes, and I would move as far away as possible from nuclear power plants. But, we don't usually see death march projects of this kind; it's more likely to be the payroll system for the nuclear power facility, or the airline reservation system used by the airline. Payroll systems and airline reservation systems aren't supposed to fail either, but the immediate consequences of a failure aren't as serious.

In any case, *perfect* reliability, maintainability, portability, etc., are not necessary, practical, or even desirable in most death march projects. Indeed, perfection isn't possible even in normal projects—it's just that we can afford to set our standards much higher because we usually have fewer constraints on time, budget, or personnel resources. For death march projects, what the users *really* want is a system that's cheap enough, fast enough, feature-rich enough, stable enough, and available soon enough—that's their definition of "good enough."

Why do we fail to achieve "good enough" software? It's usually because of a combination of the following reasons:

- We have a tendency to define quality *only* in terms of defects, without thinking about other aspects of quality—which include, from the user's perspective, the "quality" associated with having the system ready for use on a certain date.

- We assume that fewer defects = better quality, and we assume that "mo' better" quality is *always* preferred by user—even though there are circumstances when the user would be willing to trade off some defects in return for an earlier delivery, or a product that runs on a wider variety of hardware/software platforms, etc.

- We tend to define quality (defect) objectives *once*, at the beginning of the project, and keep it fixed, even though circumstances change dynamically throughout the project.

- We've been told for such a long time that *processes* are crucial, that we often forget that processes are "neutral"—a fool with a "process tool" is still a fool. You don't get quality by blindly following the details of structured analysis *or* the recommendations of SEI-CMM.

- We pursue quality with a *fixed* process that we define once, at the beginning of the project (or, even worse, for all projects in the whole company).

- We underestimate the non-linear trade-offs between such key parameters as staff size, schedule, budget, and defects—all of which are key issues for death march projects.

- We ignore the dynamics of the processes: time-delays, feedback loops, etc. Heavy overtime by the project team this week may appear to increase productivity and advance the progress of the overall project; but, it can lead to more bugs next week (something the end user and senior management may not be aware of), which will lower next week's productivity (in terms of productive output), and perhaps set the project even further behind.

- We ignore the "soft factors" associated with the process like morale, adequacy of office space, etc.

How do we achieve "good enough" software? As James Bach [12] points out, it requires several things:

- A *utilitarian strategy*—the art of qualitatively analyzing and maximizing net positive consequences in an ambiguous situation—encompassing ideas from systems thinking, risk management, economics, decision theory, game theory, control theory, and fuzzy logic.

- *An evolutionary strategy*—not only with regard to the project life cycle, but also an evolutionary view of our people, processes, and resources.
- *Heroic teams*—not the Mighty Morphin Genius Programmers, but ordinary, skillful people collaborating effectively.
- *Dynamic infrastructure*—the antithesis of bureaucracy and power politics. Upper management pays attention to projects, pays attention to the market, identifies and resolves conflicts between projects, and allows the project to "win" when there are conflicts between projects and organizational bureaucracy.
- *Dynamic processes*—processes that support work in an evolving, collaborative environment. Dynamic processes are ones you can always question because every dynamic process is part of an identifiable meta-process.

5.5 BEST PRACTICES AND WORST PRACTICES

On more than one occasion in this book, I've warned about the dangers of allowing the Methodology Police to impose a set of rigid methodologies or software processes upon a death march project team. The same advice holds for external consultants, gurus, witch doctors, faith healers, snake-oil salesmen, and textbooks. Even *this* textbook: If I've recommended something that doesn't make sense and that the project team can't carry out with enthusiasm and sincerity, then ignore it!

But, this is particularly true of methodologies and software processes. Rather than following a set of practices that somebody else has recommended—or even worse, a set of practices imposed in a top-down fashion by managers and methodology committees who usually don't know what they're talking about—it's far better to follow a set of practices that the team itself regards as "best" for the circumstances. That's the essence of the "best practices" approach that has been gaining popularity in the past couple of years: a grass-roots approach to identifying, documenting, and evangelizing software development organizations that *real developers* have found successful.

Unfortunately, death march project teams often don't have much to go on, because theirs is often regarded as the first such project within the organization. Or even if it isn't the first one, it's still regarded as an exception—so nobody has bothered cataloging the techniques that worked and the techniques that didn't. Even worse, death march projects tend to have a high mortality rate (otherwise, they wouldn't be called "death march" in the first place!). Thus, the people who would be most likely to provide useful advice for the next such project have quit, been fired, committed suicide, suffered a nervous breakdown, or have withdrawn into a shell of cynicism.

If you are indeed embarking upon the first death march project the organization has seen, then it's likely that the best you can do is document whatever practices and processes have worked in your project, for the benefit of the next death march that follows. One way of doing this is by conducting a "project audit" at the end of the project. This rarely occurs, however, and the results are usually so boring that nobody bothers reading it. The reasons are obvious: as mentioned earlier, the project team is so exhausted, frustrated, and frazzled by the end of the project that the notion of documenting their experiences is likely to be met with hoots of scorn; furthermore, many of the most valuable contributors have long since disappeared by the end of the project.

Thus, what you should consider as an alternative is a series of "mini-audits" throughout the project. If you have mini-milestones (sometimes known as "inch-pebbles") such as delivering a new version of a prototype to the user, schedule a half-day mini-audit immediately after the inch-pebble. Decide on which practices worked well, and which were disasters? What should be emphasized more heavily for the next inch-pebble, and what should be abandoned? The point here is that this kind of self-reflection is useful for the project team itself; the fact that it will also be helpful to future death march project teams is icing on the cake. Also, the team is usually in better spirits during these intermediate inch-pebble meetings, and their comments are likely to be fresher, more candid, and yet less cynical.

For the organizations that have no best-practices material available, I'll recommend a few sources. I covered the topic in one chapter of my *Rise and Resurrection of the American Programmer*; you should also look at the World Wide Web site maintained by consultant Christine Comaford at http://www.christine.com for another collection of best-practice material. Perhaps the most ambitious project underway today is the Airlie Council's efforts within the U.S. Defense Department; you can find this information on the Web at http://spmn.com.

I've listed below the "principal best practices" that the Airlie Council has recommended. Remember my earlier advice *not* to adopt this kind of information as a "stone tablet" containing "commandments" that must be followed. Rather, it could be a useful starting point for your own collection of best-practice ideas.

- *Formal risk management*—this is a concept I'll discuss later in this chapter.

- *Agreement on interfaces*—hardware interfaces, software interfaces, and interfaces between your system and other external systems.

- *Peer reviews*—inspections, walkthroughs, reviews, etc. These are commonly understood, but often rejected by death march projects, for they feel the effort will slow them down. Intellectually, most of us agree that peer reviews are beneficial, but given the kind of pressure we see in death march projects, there's a tendency for everyone to hunker down and churn out his or her own work, without bothering to have it reviewed by other team members.

- *Metric-based scheduling and management*—this says that we should base our schedules and estimates on metrics derived from previous projects. But as noted earlier, there may not have been any previous death march projects, and if there were any, it's unlikely that anyone bothered recording any useful metrics (other than a body count of human casualties). But, if there are any metrics available from "normal" projects, these can be used to calibrate the estimates being produced in the death march project—if only to see how hysterically optimistic those estimates really are!

- *Binary quality gates at the "inch-pebble" level*—i.e., rather than having milestones every three months, during which the project team reports that they're 97 percent done with all coding, there should be weekly, or even *daily* inch-pebbles with "binary" indications of progress. One means of accomplishing this is the "daily build" strategy discussed later in this chapter.

- *Project-wide visibility of project plan and progress vs. plan*—this is consistent with my recommendations in earlier chapters. Things are tough enough in a death march project without having the manager hide the status from the rest of the team.

- *Defect tracking against quality targets*—one of the ideas here is that defects identified, tracked, and resolved *early* in the development process cannot only give an indication of the defect levels in the final delivered system, but can also eliminate defects when they are relatively inexpensive, rather than waiting until the system testing stage of the project

- *Configuration management*—whether this is called version control, source code management, or some other term, it's usually regarded as an essential practice in most high-pressure projects.

- *People-aware management accountability*—alas, this is something that most death march projects *don't* pay enough attention to; as mentioned earlier, many death march projects are set up as suicide missions or kamikaze-style projects.

One of the most important contributions of the Airlie Council is the notion of *worst practices*; this is particularly applicable to death march projects, where it's often more important to avoid disasters than it is to find the best possible way to do things. The Airlie Council's list is summarized below:

- *Don't expect schedule compression of ≥10% compared to the statistical norm for similar projects*—of course, if you really believed this one, you wouldn't even start a death march project!

- *Don't justify new technology by the need for schedule compression*— you've got enough problems in a death march project without debugging new tools and technology by using beta versions of software from your friendly tool vendor. I'll discuss this in more detail in Chapter 6.

- *Don't force customer-specific implementation solutions on the project*— useful advice for *any* project

- *Don't advocate the use of silver bullet approaches*—something worth remembering when your management proposes (right after they've been visited by a persuasive vendor!) that your project can be "saved" by some new fangled tool or development methodology

- *Don't miss an opportunity to move items that are under external control off the critical path*—if your project team can't control it, then having it on the critical path makes it all the more risky. This applies to things like vendor tools, hardware boxes, software packages, and other components from external vendors. It also applies to both tangible deliverables and political decisions made by various shareholders and stakeholders surrounding the project.

- *Don't expect to achieve an accurate view of project health from a formal review attended by a large number of unprepared, active reviewers*—the project team doesn't have to worry about this, for they already *know* that such review sessions are political rituals. This advice is aimed more at the senior managers who watch the death march project from a safe distance, trying to find out whether it's in trouble.

- *Don't expect to recover from a schedule slip of ≥10 percent without a ≥10 percent reduction in software functionality to be delivered*—this is crucial advice for a death march team, because there's a good chance that the schedule *will* slip by more than 10 percent during the course of the project. Indeed, even a 10 percent slippage is dangerous in a death march project, for the team is probably already working so much overtime that they don't have the additional capacity to work 10 percent *more* hours in each day. But, the main point of this suggestion from the Airlie Council is to remind the project manager that people-time and software-functionality are not exchangeable in a linear fashion.

During the past year, I've posed two questions to several hundred software managers in seminar audiences around the world: "If a colleague of yours was about to embark upon a death march project, what is the *one thing* that you would advise him/her to do in order to succeed? And what is the one thing you would advise him/her *not* to do?" I've been intrigued to find that *nobody* has *ever* identified tools or technology as the "one most important thing," nor has anyone mentioned formal methods or techniques such as structured analysis or object-oriented design. A few people have recommended peopleware strategies (e.g., "hire good people," and "make sure that the team is really committed to succeed"), but almost all of the recommendations have centered on the issue of negotiations, scope management (which is handled well by the triage concept discussed earlier), and risk management (which I'll discuss below).

One last concept from the Airlie Council might be useful for death march projects, though it's likely to be used more by the managers *outside* the project than the manager or team members *inside* the project. It's called the "breathalyzer test": What questions should you ask a death march project team to quickly determine whether it was so out of touch with reality that it should be shut down? These are also the sort of questions that consultants often ask when they are commissioned by senior management to review the status of a project. I've been in that position myself, and I can usually tell the project is in trouble when I see the glazed eyes of the project manager, who looks like a deer caught in the headlights of an onrushing car.

Sometimes a question like "Do you know who your customer is? Do you know who you're supposed to deliver this stuff to?" leads to an embarrassed silence, while everyone on the project team looks blankly at one another and then stares at the floor. But, if you need some more breathalyzer test questions, here's the list from the Airlie Council:

- Do you have a current, credible activity network supported by a Work Breakdown Structure (WBS)?
- Do you have a current, credible schedule and budget?
- Do you know what software you are responsible for delivering?
- Can you list the top ten project risks?
- Do you know your schedule compression percentage?
- What is the estimated size of your software deliverable? How was it derived?
- Do you know the percentage of external interfaces that are not under your control?
- Does your staff have sufficient expertise in the project domain?

- Have you identified adequate staff to allocate to the various tasks at the scheduled time?

As mentioned earlier, the reason the breathalyzer test is administered is that someone in the organization—usually *not* the project manager, but someone much higher in the management ranks—has a "gut feeling" that the project is in trouble. For their own political survival, the project manager and the entire team should ask the same questions of one another periodically. And, the project manager should be on the lookout for other signs that the project is in trouble even when things look okay on the official PERT chart:

- Key project team members are quitting—this may occur for a number of reasons, but it's important to get a sense of whether team members are losing faith in their ability to finish the project. If key members begin quitting, others may follow.
- The "inverse Dilbert correlation factor"—the more Dilbert cartoons pasted on office doors and bulletin boards, the less well off the project is.
- Excessive gallows humor—if the project team begins wearing black shirts to the office, or piping funeral dirges through the Muzak system, you're in trouble.
- New names for the project, e.g., "Project Titanic"—another form of gallows humor, but usually a more serious indication that the project team has lost faith, lost respect, and lost any real interest in whether the project will ever succeed.
- An ominous silence from end users and senior management, who used to ask on a daily basis how the project was coming along—by the time you recognize this, it may be too late to recover, but you should have at least a few days to update your resume.
- Thrashing—lots of activity but no sign of forward progress. Avoiding this is what the "inch-pebble" idea and the "daily build" strategy are all about.

5.6 THE "DAILY BUILD" CONCEPT

In the discussion about prototyping, milestones, and inch-pebbles above, there was an unspoken assumption that the incremental "deliverables" produced by the project team would appear at intervals measured in months or weeks. That's what most of us are accustomed to from our past experience with "normal" projects, and it's consistent with the usual pace of business life—e.g., weekly staff meetings, monthly status reviews, quarterly presentations to senior management, etc.

But, death march projects, as we've seen throughout this book, typically need a different approach. When it comes to prototyping and incremental development, it often makes sense to organize the entire project around the concept of a "daily build." By this, I mean: compile, link, install, and test the entire collection of code produced by the team *every day*, as if this was the last day before the deadline and you had to ship whatever you've got to the user tomorrow morning.

Realistically, you can't start the daily build on the first day of the project. And while it might be possible to build the equivalent of a "Hello World" subroutine on the second day of the project, it won't impress anyone unless *everything* about the project involves completely new technology (e.g., many of the Java-based projects that are underway as this book is being written in 1996). But, there's usually a point well before the first "official" demonstration or delivery of a prototype version of the system when the software developers have a reasonable collection of components, subroutines, or modules—at least a few hundred lines of code, and perhaps a few thousand lines—that actually accepts real input, does real calculations or processing, and produces real output. That's the point when the daily build should begin, and a new (and hopefully better) version of the system should be built every day thereafter.

Why is this so important? As Jim McCarthy, Microsoft's Visual C++ product manager and author of *Dynamics of Software Development* [13], likes to say, "The daily build is the heartbeat of the project. It's how you know you're alive." And, there can hardly be a more important priority for the manager of a death march project. If a week goes by when everyone is spinning their wheels and nobody has quite had the nerve to tell the project manager that they just can't manage to get the newfangled object-oriented database to communicate properly with the client-server application they're working on, the project may have fallen hopelessly behind schedule. As long as the project manager hears status reports delivered in a verbal fashion, or documented in written memos (or with data flow diagrams), it's all too easy to confuse motion with progress, and effort with achievement. But, if the project manager insists on physically observing the behavior of each day's "daily build," it's much more difficult to hide whatever problems are plaguing the project.

Some project managers will nod their heads and confirm that this is how they've *always* done it; but, most will admit that they've settled for weekly builds, or monthly builds, or semi-annual releases of a system. While nobody can rightly claim to have "invented" the concept, many feel that Dave Cutler should be given the credit for popularizing it during the development of the Windows NT operating system (an interesting discussion can be found in Greg Zachary's *Show Stopper!* [14] description of the project). It's also interesting to note that Microsoft's Windows 95 development project also used the daily build concept; the final beta version before the production system was released in August 1995 was known as "Build 951."

It's important to recognize that an approach like this effectively becomes part of the project team's *process* for developing the system. Imagine what it must be like to be part of a team that must demonstrate a working version of its software on 951 consecutive days! [15] Furthermore, to be effective, the daily build should be automated, and should run unattended in the middle of the night, when all of the programmers have gone home (or have climbed under their desks and into their sleeping bags!). This implies the existence of automated configuration management and source code control mechanisms, as well as automated "scripts" of some kind to carry out the compiling and linking activities. But most importantly, it implies the existence of an automated test management system that can run all night long, pounding away on the new version of code to see if it still runs yesterday's test cases properly. Thus, to make the daily build concept work, it's almost certain that a reasonable set of tools and technology are readily available; we'll discuss this in Chapter 6.

A few small tricks can add even more value to the daily build concept:

- The project manager should move his or her office to the test site, or operation center, once the daily build process begins. Dave Cutler did this at Microsoft, and there are apocryphal stories of the tantrums that he threw when he arrived at the office and found that the daily build had crashed in the middle of the night. Tantrums or not, the point is that the project manager wants to be *very* visible, and *very* involved in the daily build process, rather than being the commanding general at the rear of the army, receiving daily reports on a battle taking place miles away.

- Since it's likely that the daily build will require at least a small amount of manual supervision while it runs in the middle of the night, it may help to establish the following policy: Any programmer whose buggy code causes the daily build to crash gets the honor of supervising the operation of the (nightly) daily build until the next victim causes a crash. Obviously, there are advantages and disadvantages of such a policy, but at the very least, it makes the whole concept of the daily build much more "real" to the project team!

- Assign one of the programmers who normally comes into the office early in the morning the task of checking whether the daily build ran successfully, and then posting the results in a visible place. If nobody is willing or able to show up early, then hire a college student. One company instructed the student to plant a flag outside the building to warn everyone whether it was going to be a good day or bad day when they arrived: a green flag meant the daily build had succeeded, while a red flag meant that it had failed.

5.7 RISK MANAGEMENT

If requirements management—particularly the triage prioritization of requirements—is the most important process within a death march project, the second most important is *risk management*. If "risk" weren't such a critical issue, we wouldn't apply the adjective "death march" to the project. It's interesting to note that one of the breathalyzer test questions identified by the Airlie Council is concerned with identification of project risks; and while that question might draw a blank stare from the manager of a "normal" project (even if that normal project has gotten into terrible trouble), it's one that can typically be answered fairly crisply by the manager of a death march project. A manager would be a fool if he or she initiated a death march without having had some serious thought about the primary risks and how they might be mitigated.

Alas, things sometimes get out of hand as the death march project continues. That is, because the risk management activity is addressed in terms of ad hoc emotions and instinct rather than as a formal process, the manager often misses the emergence of new risks as the project continues. In the best case, the risks that were visible at the beginning of the project will be eliminated; in the normal case, they continue to be worrisome risks throughout the project (e.g., the risk that a key team member will quit). But, entirely new risks—things that nobody anticipated—can suddenly emerge, and because the team typically has very little "slack" or "reserve" capacity, in terms of schedule, budget, and resources, these new risks can be killers.

If this whole discussion of software risks strikes you as excessive or irrelevant, feel free to skip to the next chapter. My biggest concern is for the project manager who has survived several "normal" projects with an intuitive, ad hoc risk management approach; that usually won't work in a death march project. Indeed, it's the existence of an effective, formal Software Risk Management (SRM) *process* that makes some organizations willing to "go out on a limb" and take on a death march project that would otherwise be certain suicide.

There is a substantial body of literature on risk management, and it's beyond the scope of this book to cover it all. The references at the end of this chapter [16,17,18,19] will provide as much detail as you need, though it's important here too to avoid having the "risk management police" overwhelm the project with forms, reports, and other aspects of bureaucracy. For example, some death march project managers follow a very simple process of having the team identify and monitor the *top ten* risks in the project; these can be printed on a one-page form, and their status can be quickly reviewed on a weekly basis.

Obviously, other approaches can work just as well; but, the key is to ensure that it's one that will be understood, accepted, and followed by everyone on the project team—for it's the peons at the bottom of the hierarchy who are usually the first to see the emergence of new risks. In a death march project, we don't have time to let the information trickle up to the top of the management hierarchy by whatever antiquated communication mechanisms are used to convey other forms of political information; the risks must be pounced on and attacked by the team as a whole to prevent them from getting out of control.

The word "control" is crucial here, for the project team must distinguish between risk *assessment*, risk *control*, and risk *avoidance*. In the worst case, the project team reacts to risks as they occur—e.g., by allocating additional resources for additional testing to alleviate the consequences of a bug. This kind of "fix on failure" approach, where the risks are addressed *after* they have surfaced, often leads to a crisis-mode form of "fire fighting" that can lead to utter collapse of the death march project team. Risk *prevention* is usually far better, and it means that the team agrees to follow a formal process of assessment and control to preclude potential risks from occurring.

An even more proactive form of risk management seeks to eliminate the root causes of failures and risk; this is often the focus of quality management initiatives within an organization. It tends to expand the scope of risk assessment to a broader horizon, to allow the *anticipation* of risks, and it can lead to a very aggressive management culture, which incorporates a "risk-taking" ethic by *engineering* the degree of risk that the organization can tolerate. I'm all in favor of such an approach, but it's a more strategic issue than ought to be discussed and implemented outside the context of a death march project. The death march project team has a very tactical perspective: It's not trying to change the culture of the organization, but merely survive and finish the project.

However, this may involve some culture problems in the organization, especially if there is a perception that *other* projects have not been risky, and that this one is the first, last, and only death march project the organization will ever see. The problem is that the project team is not an island unto itself; if it were, then it could simply focus on the cultural problem of "shooting the messenger" who reports problems to higher-level authorities.

But, as Rob Charette observes [20], the major causes of project failures often exist in the organizational environment, and/or in the business environment, which surround the project; this is illustrated in Figure 5.2. The organizational and business environments are almost always outside the project manager's jurisdiction and political control; but equally important, the project manager often doesn't know about these "external" risks until they come crashing into his or her project.

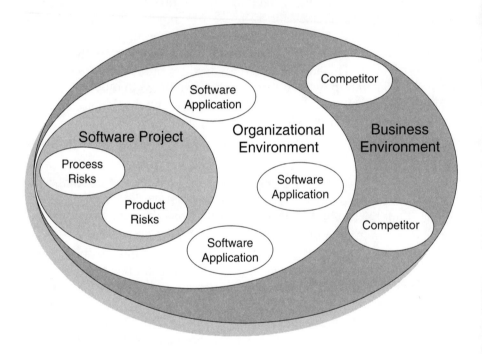

FIGURE 5.2 THE SCOPE OF PROJECT RISKS

Of course, the converse can be true also: The software project creates risks that can affect the organization and external business environment. But, everyone knows that! Indeed, the project manager can expect to be reminded *ad nauseam* that the entire organization—if not civilization, and the entire universe!—is imperiled by the death march project. But, these same managers, who whine and complain about the fact that the project team is only working 127 hours per week to get the project finished, are often blissfully unaware of things going on in their sphere of control which could de-rail the death march project.

That's why it's important to have a risk management process that can assess project risks from several different organizational perspectives and balance them appropriately; after all, what engineering (and the software developers) sees as a risk might be seen as an opportunity by the marketing department. This kind of "global" view of risk management is important, but I don't see it as often as I would like when I visit death march projects. And as noted above, the project team doesn't have the time, energy, or political clout to change the organizational culture by installing a global risk management process. Thus, the absence of such an organizational process becomes a risk of its own, which the team must assess.

Risk *assessment* is usually performed by evaluating the complexity of the system or product being developed, as well as evaluating the client and project team environments. Product complexity can be assessed in terms of size (e.g., number of function points), performance constraints, technical complexity, etc. Risks associated with the client environment are often a factor of the number of user constituencies involved, the level of user knowledge, the perceived importance of the system within the user's business area, the likelihood that when/if the new system is installed it will lead to a reorganization or downsizing activity, etc. And, the risks associated with the team environment include the capabilities, experience, morale, and physical/emotional health of the project team.

Typically, there are a hundred or more risk factors that could be included in a comprehensive risk model; as noted earlier, some project teams will consciously narrow their focus to just the top ten risks. Some of the risks can be quantified in an objective fashion—e.g., the response-time performance requirements, or the size of the system in function points. But other factors—e.g., the degree of user cooperation or hostility—may have to be assessed on a qualitative basis. As a practical management approach, it's usually appropriate to categorize such risks as "high," "low," or "medium" and to focus on getting a consensus on the state, or level, of the risk on the part of everyone involved.

Once the risks have been identified and assessed, the manager and the team can sometimes identify appropriate strategies to minimize or eliminate as many as possible. This is common sense, of course, but it must be remembered that the very nature of a death march project is that there are usually more than the usual number of risks, and that they're more severe, and they *cannot* be eliminated through simple actions. On the other hand, if the risks are extraordinary, sometimes the solutions are too: While the project team might never have dared to ask the CEO or Senior Vice President to eliminate a project risk on a normal project by spending an extraordinary sum of money or eliminating a severe bureaucratic constraint, it's not unreasonable to ask for such things in a death march project. And if you don't ask—which will often require going around the chain of command, and circumventing several levels of brain-dead middle managers—then you'll never know whether you could have acquired the solution to your problems.

In any case, if there are high risk factors that cannot be summarily eliminated—which is almost always the situation in a death march project—then they should be documented with a "risk memorandum" that identifies the risk impact, the possible higher-level actions, the contingency plans that need to be set in place, etc. This is not just a "cover your ass" political act, for if the risks do materialize, and if they cause the project to fail, there will usually be dire consequences for everyone involved; after all, that's part of the reality of a death march project. However, *denying* reality is also a common phenomenon on death march projects. It's common for both members of the project team, and for the various levels of users and managers surrounding the team to put on their blindfolds and steadfastly ignore the existence of serious project risks. It's not unreasonable to expect the project manager and team members to focus on "internal" risks with extreme diligence; but as noted earlier, the "external" risks often can't be controlled by the team members, because they're associated with organizational or business issues beyond their jurisdiction. Thus, a risk memorandum is an important *practical* activity, to force the user and management communities to acknowledge what they would prefer to overlook and ignore.

5.8 SUMMARY

It's all too easy to go overboard with many of the ideas that I've discussed in this chapter, and thus fall into the deadly trap of mind-numbing, time-wasting bureaucracy. But, as Stephen Nesbitt reminded me in an e-mail message [21] that arrived just as I had reached the end of this chapter without a clever way of bringing things to an end:

> ...the absence of standards and methodology can also turn a project into a Death March. On my last project for example, the unrealistic delivery schedule was used as an excuse to avoid the following:
>
> 1) Checking source code into the configuration management system resulting in project source code spread across 3 different computer systems at 2 geographic locations. As a consequence a significant amount of time was wasted trying:
>
> > a) to build the software.
> >
> > b) to determine who had what version.
> >
> > c) to determine why the software worked on one system and not another.
>
> 2) Registering features/defects into the configuration management system. This effectively crippled QA because it was impossible to easily determine what was in work and could be ignored, what was completed and could be tested, and what was pending so that appropriate test plans could be designed.
>
> 3) Recording basic requirements, design decisions and assumptions, milestones *within* the development of project modules, and appropriate unit tests. The consequence here was to drastically impede communications within the project team not only on current project status but also basic decisions made at the beginning of the project.

> Inevitably development response was that these pro-
> cess activities represented "overhead" and thus, by
> definition, were *useless* activities. Technical manage-
> ment generally concurred and, when the drop dead
> date loomed, process and methodology were given the
> heave ho.

So, please don't interpret this chapter as an excuse not to have any processes, methods, or techniques at all; indeed, that will kill a death march project, too! The trick is to find the ones that matter, the ones that work, and the ones that the team will follow naturally and unconsciously. This last point is crucial: the team will be under a lot of stress and pressure, and will have to do a lot of things by instinct. If they are overburdened with new, unfamiliar processes so complex that they have to stop every five minutes and consult a textbook to figure out what to do, then all is lost. So keep it simple—and if the team can only remember one word, remember what it is: *triage.*

Notes/References

1. Stephen R. Covey, A. Roger Merrill, and Rebecca R. Merrill, *First Things First* (New York: Simon & Schuster, 1994).

2. Consultant John Boddie suggests a third option: The new manager might be the one to officially kill the project if it really is unsalvageable. This is much easier for the new manager than for his or her predecessor, for the original project manager has so much ego and emotion invested in the project that it's difficult for him or her to admit that the best thing to do is kill the project. Boddie provides some excellent advice on politically acceptable ways to kill a project in "Calling Doctor Kevorkian!" *American Programmer*, February 1997.

3. Indeed, I would suggest that the project manager and his or her team members use this as a litmus test at the beginning of the project. If the user, project owner, senior managers, shareholders, and stakeholders all refuse to accept the notion of this kind of hard-nosed *triage* prioritization, then the most rational thing to do is resign from the project before things get any worse! As a further litmus test, Dean Leffingwell argues that the users should be required to divide the entire set of requirements into equal groups of three: one third of the requirements can be put into the "must-do" category, one-third into the "should-do" category, and one-third into the "could-do" category. This prevents the common problem of finding that 90 percent of the requirements have been categorized as critical.

4. This is a preview of a more elaborate discussion of "best practices" that you'll find later in this chapter.

5. By contrast, in a "normal" project, the SA/OOA models are often perceived as useful products in their own right. The users and business policy-makers will huddle around the data flow diagrams and mutter to one another, "So *that's* what our business is all about! Maybe we should do a business reengineering project and change all of that before we build a new software system!"

6. Veteran software engineers will recall the old adage, "If your only tool is a hammer, then all the problems facing you look like nails."

7. I must confess that this is a disguised marketing pitch, since it's one of the key features of the Requisite product, and I was a member of Requisite's Board when I wrote this book. In my role as an objective author, I heartily encourage you to investigate all three requirements management products mentioned here.

8. Ed,
> 1. How important is it to use traditional methodologies like SA/
SD > or OOA/OOD in a death-march project?
I'd have thought that they can contribute to the deathmarch more
effectively than most. On one project I know, they needed a
diagrammer for the ERDs, so they bought Excellerator. Having found
that it supported SSADM (which must be the methodologist's
methodology) adopted it without any training or induction for the
staff. Then they found that the pace of the project slowed
significantly (in fact, it nearly halted) while everyone was busy
reading manuals and learning software tools and deciding what they
should do next (and re-doing what they had done earlier in the
"wrong" sequence). For death march watchers, and almost ideal
scenario. Oh, and the project manager was sacked half way through
the project, but that's normal.
> How important is it to teach those methodologies (whichever one
 > you think is best) to the team before the project begins?
Well, I guess you can gather from the above that I believe in
training for ANYTHING before applying it. The fact that you're
adopting a technique which will fundamentally decide the way you
work, record all your requirements, and govern the nature of the
generated code, you'd think that a slight amount of training would
be beneficial, wouldn't you? A lot of training would be better, of
course. But when you're on a death march, you don't have time for
that.

A little sideline quote that I received from a Systems Manager the
other day: I said I wanted to spend the first nine months of the
project getting the design right, and he responded by saying "You
can't do that - you've got to deliver the Name and Address file in
twelve months." (!) It's not a death march. It's not a death march.
It's not a death march. Yet.

> 3. How important is the SEI-CMM or ISO-9000 or any other "formal"
> software process approach within the context of a death march
> project team?

Not at all, I'd say. I don't know SEI-CMM, apart from what I've
seen here, but ISO-9000 is self-certified, so it doesn't pose a
problem here at all. If it does, you hire a specialist whose job
is to cook the books.

> 4. Almost all death march projects follow a RAD or prototyping
> approach

Well, what's worse is that suddenly when people realise that the
deadline's going to slip, RAD suddenly rears its ugly head.
Obviously, RAD is all about tightly constrained environments,
whereas the death march is plagued by vague or exaggerated
requirements. I can't see how an attempt to RAD a death march can
succeed, unless you turn it into producing a "navigable model" or
some such prototype so as to get the management off your back.

> 5. If you could only get the project team to focus on ONE process
> approach, what would it be?

For me, it's all working in small teams, tightly focussed, and each
one delivering *something*, so there's an end in sight. Checking
each others' work is the other aspect I'd introduce. Not
necessarily walkthroughs (although that's a more formal part of
it), but simply ensuring that someone else who is knowledgeable
can help with any task. Share the workload, the problems, and the
vision.

> 6. If there was one kind of process approach that you would
> strongly advise the death march project to AVOID

Large user groups (such as a Model Office) who have control of the
design. If the number of users involved is too great, the business
will give you only those it can spare, and they will continually
argue amongst themselves because they don't know. We've had to pull
a project to a dead halt while we pulled in some senior users to
go through all the requirements and sort out the wheat from the
chaff. Meanwhile 60 implementors twiddled their thumbs for a couple
of weeks.

> 7. How important is all of this process stuff, in comparison to
> the issues of peopleware

People, people, and people - the three most important things you
need on any project. Get the best and keep them, and lose the rest.
You can work with a team one-third the size of what you think if
they're good, and if they're that good, they'll adopt a common,
useful process. So process is important, but good people come
first, and when they're that good, they'll adopt good practices
which aren't a drag on the project.

Tools/technology come ahead of processes, I believe, and it's the
one thing the managers can do for their staff that can help
significantly.

--Doug

9. Ed

>> 2. What if the death march project team has never used such
methodologies before? How important is it to teach those
methodologies (whichever one you think is best) to the team before
the project begins? <<

Is there any time at all "before the project begins"?
A death march project is not the time for staff to learn a new (or
their first) methodology. OTOH it would contribute greatly to the
chances of project death if they DID learn a new methodology at
the same time.

Paul

10. Ed,

>> 1. How important is it to use traditional methodologies like
SA/SD or OOA/OOD in a death march project?<<

It can't hurt to have clear ways of communicating with the users
and clear deliverables to them.

>>2. What if the death march project team has never used such
methodologies before? How important is it to teach those
methodologies (whichever one you think is best) to the team before
the project begins?<<

It depends on whether members of the team have the experience that
the team as a whole lacks. I'd say that the core members need to
"know their stuff" for the most part.

>>3. How important is the SEI-CMM or ISO-9000 or any other "formal"
software process approach within the context of a death march
project team? Is it better to follow an "ad hoc" approach, and just
assume that the pressures of a death march will force everyone to
operate as a "cowboy" programmer? ("cowperson" would probably be
more politically correct, but it sounds too clumsy <g>)<<

Cowpokes don't need the manure to be cleaned from the pasture.

Programmers don't need to have the "methodology" gurus clean up the deliverables.

But if someone wants to have a formal software process, then the folks doing the programming should be protected from that extra effort.

>>4. Almost all death march projects follow a RAD or prototyping approach to systems development (or spiral, or scrum, or iterative, or various other related ideas) instead of the old-fashioned waterfall approach. That point hardly seems worth emphasizing -- but are there any special caveats or exceptions or details about RAD/prototyping/etc. that you would be sure that a death march project manager understood?<<

Understand this: the feedback that you got from the user is critical. They don't care how you meet their requirements, and if they have seen "early miracles" of pretty screens and promised functionality, don't ever let them down.

>>5. If you could only get the project team to focus on ONE process approach, what would it be? Walkthroughs? Change management (aka version control, configuration management, etc.)? formal analysis/ design methodologies? something else?<<

Walkthoughs or reviews with the key (or a few key) user(s)? I really think that one of the more major problems of systems projects is that there is a cycle of delivery and failure to satisfy.

>>6. If there was one kind of process approach that you would strongly advise the death march project to AVOID (because it takes too much time, is too risky, or whatever), what would it be?<<

Anything that is extremely complex and technical and theoretical is wasted on a death march. Nobody can see further than the next deliverable.

>>7. How important is all of this process stuff, in comparison to the issues of peopleware (which I discussed in Chapter 4), and tools/technology (which I'll get to in Chapter 6)? <<

The tools are useful, but they should only illustrate and enable. The process is a means of getting to the human side of the effort. The peopleware is the most important.

Sharon

11. Watts Humphrey, *A Discipline of Software Engineering* (Reading, MA: Addison-Wesley, 1995).

12. James Bach, "The Challenge of 'Good Enough' Software," *American Programmer*, October 1995.

13. Jim McCarthy, *Dynamics of Software Development* (Redmond, WA: Microsoft Press, 1995).

14. G. Pascal Zachary, *Show-Stopper!* (New York: Free Press, 1994).

15. To be honest, I don't know if the Microsoft team actually did this religiously on a daily basis. It's certainly possible that more than one "build" was produced within a single 24-hour period, and it's even possible that the team took a day or two off during their marathon death march.

16. See Note 13.

17. See Note 14.

18. Rob Thomsett, "The Indiana Jones School of Risk Management," *American Programmer*, September 1992.

19. Capers Jones, *Assessment and Control of Software Risks*, (Englewood Cliffs, NJ: Prentice Hall, 1994).

20. Rob Charette, "Building Bridges over Intellectual Rivers," *American Programmer*, September 1992.

21. Ed:

> Three weeks ago I was 35 year old [xxx] systems engineer providing quality assurance services on an ugly Death March project here in Bozeman, MT. I'm still 35 but I resigned my position because, after 18 months, the stress, despair and lack of job satisfaction were simply too much to take. With no dependents I could afford to simply walk away even if it is financially uncomfortable.
>
> As such, I am finding your draft chapters for Death March particularly relevant as I try to understand what happened over the last 18 months, and as I start the process of looking for an employer where Death Marches are not the norm (or at least not ugly or suicidal ones!)
>
> In reading Chapter 2 you made a number of references to the "methodology police" as one of the factors which can turn a project into a Death March - the implication being that methodology and standards can cripple an already marginal project. I think this is absolutely true. I am bothered, however, that the converse was not mention that the absence of standards and methodology can also turn a project into a Death March.
>
> On my last project for example, the unrealistic delivery schedule was used as an excuse to avoid the following:
>
> 1) Checking source code into the configuration management system resulting in project source code spread across 3 different computer

systems at 2 geographic locations. As a consequence a significant amount of time was
wasted trying:
a) to build the software.
b) to determine who had what version.
c) to determine why the software worked on one system and not another.
2) Registering features/defects into the configuration management system. This effectively crippled QA because it was impossible to easily determine what was in work and could be ignored, what was completed and could be tested, and what was pending so that appropriate test plans could be designed.
3) Recording basic requirements, design decisions and assumptions, milestones _within_ the development of project modules, and appropriate unit tests. The consequence here was to drastically impede communications within the project team not only on current project status but also basic decisions made at the beginning of the project. Inevitably development response was that these process activities represented "overhead" and thus, by definition, were _useless_ activities. Technical management generally concurred and, when the drop dead date loomed, process and methodology were given the heave ho.
The results were significant:
1) One system was finally put into production 1 year after delivery. That additional year was spent correcting significant design and implementation flaws which, in addition to requiring massive amounts of engineering
resources, also resulted in millions of dollars of fines.
2) One system was put in production with three brand new, never tested
systems. The result was the need to dedicate engineering resources for a period of one month to provide continuous around the clock supervision. It also led to the general perception by the customer that the system was not working - a perception that has not yet been changed.
3) One system was put in and totally failed leading to:
a) $20 million dollars in fines on a $35 million contract.
b) Loss of another multimillion dollar contract.
c) Removal of the system by the customer.
Perhaps a little methodology would not have made any difference. On the other hand, how could it have made things worse?
I hope that the final form of Death March will address this very issue recognizing that absence of _appropriate_ methodologies can

transform a project into a Death March just as completely as the
overzealous application of _inappropriate_ processes,
methodologies and standards. As a battle weary infantry man, I also
hope that the final book will provide insight into recognizing the
appropriate from the inappropriate.
Thanks for your time, and I apologize for the length of my post.
Enjoy your summer along Flathead Lake.
-steve

Additional References

Alan M. Davis, *Software Requirements: Objects, Functions, and States* (Englewood
Cliffs, NJ: Prentice Hall, 1993).

Mark C. Paulk, Charles V. Weber, Bill Curtis, Mary Beth Chrissis, et al., *The Capability Maturity Model: Guidelines for Improving the Software Process* (Reading,
MA: Addison-Wesley, 1995).

Robert N. Charette, *Application Strategies for Risk Analysis*, (New York: McGraw-
Hill, 1990).

Robert N. Charette, *Software Engineering Risk Analysis and Management*, (New
York: McGraw-Hill, 1989).

chapter

Tools and Technology

A worker may be the hammer's master, but the hammer still prevails.
A tool knows exactly how it is meant to be handled, while the user of
the tool can only have an approximate idea.

> **Milan Kundera,** *The Book of Laughter and Forgetting,*
>
> Pt. 7, Chapter 8 (1978; tr. 1980)

Back in the summer of 1992, I had dinner with an amiable group of mid-level Microsoft managers. During the course of the discussion, I asked if it was common for Microsoft project teams to use such methodologies as structured analysis or object-oriented design. The answers ranged from "sometimes" to "ummm, I guess so" to "not consistently" to "what's that?" And when I asked about the use of CASE tools (which were still fairly popular throughout the rest of the industry at that point in time), I was told that the common opinion of Microsofties was that such tools

175

were for "people off the street." This was a term I hadn't heard before, but the rough translation is "ignorant savages who have just come out of the primeval forest and who are just learning to program, unlike *real* programmers, who don't need no such artsy-fartsy tools."

Somewhat depressed, I asked whether the project teams used *any* tools, and was told that in fact, each Microsoft team can choose whatever tools it feels are appropriate for the project it's working on. Seizing on that, I asked: what does a typical project team consider its most *important* tool for a software project?

"I asked one of the project teams the same question the other day," replied one of the managers. "And you know what their answer was?"

"A high-speed C++ compiler?" I asked. "An assembler? A powerful debugging tool for all those bugs in their code, heh heh heh?"

"None of the above," the manager responded, ignoring my snide joke. "Their answer was: *electronic mail*. The average Microsoft programmer gets a hundred e-mail messages a day; he *lives* on e-mail. Take away e-mail and the project stops dead in its tracks."

There's a reason why I began this anecdote by pointing out that it took place in 1992: this was before the explosive growth of the Internet had begun, and before the World Wide Web was available. I was staggered at the thought of anyone getting a hundred e-mail messages a day; in 1992, I was deliriously happy if I got two or three e-mail messages a day. But as you can imagine, if the same question about "most important tool" was raised in 1996, the answer might well be "World Wide Web" rather than e-mail; by contrast, the answer might have been "fax machine" in 1987, "PC workstation" in 1983, "on-line terminal" in 1976, and "my own telephone on my desk" when I began my programming career in 1964.

Obviously, we don't expect a death march project team to survive with only one tool. Most teams—even for normal projects—have a wide variety of tools, and quite an assortment of technology, to accomplish their day-to-day work. But sometimes, they have too much, and sometimes they have technology that's too new, and sometimes they have tools they don't want foisted upon them by Dilbertesque managers. And, in some cases, they're prevented—for financial, political, or cultural reasons—from getting the one tool they believe critical for accomplishing their objectives.

In case you were worried, let me reassure you that I'm not going to advocate esoteric, advanced software tools that somehow communicate telepathically with the programmer to generate well-structured code from disorganized thoughts. But, I do want to discuss the notion of a "minimal toolset" for death march projects. I also want to emphasize the critical relationship between tools and processes, especially since the processes in a death march project are likely to be different from those used in the rest of the organization. And finally, I want to issue a warning against introducing completely *new* tools, of any kind, into a death march project team environment.

6.1 THE MINIMAL TOOLSET

In the previous chapter, I strongly recommended the notion of *triage* as a prioritization strategy for dealing with user requirements. The same concept applies to tools and technology for the project team: There are some tools the team "must have," and some that they "should have," and a bewildering variety of tools they "could have." There are also some good reasons for applying the triage prioritization in a conscious, cold-blooded fashion at the beginning of the project.

The most obvious reason is economics. Even if the tools worked and everyone was familiar with them, it would cost too much money to acquire them. And it would take too long to order them—by the time the procurement process in a normal corporate bureaucracy was finished, the project would be finished [1]. In many death march projects, it's important to focus on a few critical tools, and then try to persuade senior management (or the Tools Police) to acquire them.

But, suppose the team is operating in a large environment that already has hundreds of different tools that have been acquired over the years. Should they all be used? Obviously not! Even if they all work, the mental effort required to remember *how* they work, and the additional effort to make them all work together, usually exceeds the incremental benefit obtained. Consider the analogy of a team of mountain-climbers, trying to decide what equipment to take with them as they prepare for an assault on the peak. There are some essentials (tents, drinking water, etc.) they'd better have; and, if it's an easy climb, they might want to take along some new-fangled gadgets they read about in their favorite mountain-climbing magazine. But, if they're planning to climb Mt. Everest, without the assistance of burros or Sherpas to carry everything, then they can't afford the burden of carrying 300 pounds of gear per person on their backs.

Exactly what tools *are* critical, and what should be left behind, is a decision the death march project should be allowed to make on its own—regardless of whether it conforms to organizational standards. I'm staggered by the number of organizations I visit where the death march project manager tells me sadly that there's an organizational mandate that *all* projects be done in COBOL (or, in other organizations, Visual Basic, or Oracle, or whatever...), even though that technology is utterly inappropriate for his or her project. Baloney! Throw it out! Use the tools and technology that make sense! To do otherwise is roughly analogous to someone telling the leader of the Mt. Everest mountain-climbing team, "Our committee has decided that your project team should take along a detailed map of the New York City subway system, because most projects have found it very helpful."[2]

I think it's essential that the team members agree on common tools *within* the project; otherwise, chaos will ensue. Obviously, this must be interpreted with a certain degree of common sense; it probably doesn't matter which word processor the team members use to write their documentation, but it probably *is* important that they all use the same compiler for their C++ code. One of the problems with a death march project is that the software developers believe that it creates a license for complete anarchy at the individual level (e.g., if they want to use an obscure C++ compiler they downloaded from a university Web site, they believe it's their inalienable right). Not so: It's the *team* that has the inalienable right, and the project manager must enforce this strictly in any area where incompatible tools could make a significant difference.

This means that unless the team members have worked together on several previous death march projects, they will have to come up with a "minimal" toolset that everyone agrees to use. Thus, triage emerges again: The "must-have" toolset is also the "must-*use*" toolset. Once a consensus has emerged on a set of tools, the team can discuss the "should-have" tools, where the problems are likely to be a combination of consensus-building within the team, and management approval for the purchase of new tools. Beyond that, there may or may not be sufficient time and energy to discuss the merits of the nearly-infinite number of "could-have" tools that various team members might be interested in.

I suggested above that the project manager must be prepared to enforce the consensus; indeed, this could be one of the criteria used by the manager to select potential members of the team. Note that the same could be said about the software processes that we discussed in Chapter 6. And as we'll see below, it's even more important than that—because tools and processes are intimately related to one another.

With all of these caveats in mind, it's impossible for an "outsider" like me to casually enumerate the recommended tools for a death march project. When asked the question, my answer—"It depends..."—is usually confused for the consultant's weasel-worded tendency to avoid giving a straight answer to any question. So, as long as you keep my earlier advice firmly in mind, here is the list of tools I would normally look for:

- *E-mail, groupware, Internet/Web tools*—like the Microsoft anecdote above, this tool is at the top of my list. That's because electronic-interaction tools are not only a means for communicating much more efficiently than memos and faxes, but also because they facilitate coordination and collaboration. Basic e-mail and access to the Internet is something I would insist upon as a project manager, though I would be happy to negotiate as to *which* vendors and products should be used. It matters far less to me whether we're using Microsoft Mail, cc:Mail, Netscape Collabra, or Lotus Notes, than the concept that the whole team is on the network and keeps all of its "project memory" on the network. Beyond that, there are some wonderful new tools available, but they're likely to fall into the category of "could have" rather than "must have."

- *Prototyping/RAD development tools*—as discussed earlier, almost all death march projects use some form of prototyping or incremental development approach; consequently, they need tools to support this effort. It's hard finding a popular development environment today that describes itself as anything else *but* a RAD environment, and the majority of such tools today have a visual, drag-and-drop user interface to help the programmer get more code developed more quickly. Whether the tool should be based on Delphi, C++, Visual Basic, or Smalltalk (or a dozen other possible choices) is something I can't recommend on any kind of global basis. But remember the comment above: It's not sufficient to have a consensus that we're all going to use a language like C++ or Smalltalk; we have to agree on a common toolset from a common vendor. To have part of the team using ParcPlace-Digitalk's VisualWorks environment while the others use IBM's VisualAge for Smalltalk product may be technologically feasible, but it's still downright stupid.

- *Configuration Management (CM)/version control*—Several of my colleagues feel that this should be at the top of the list. As John Boddie, author of *Crunch Mode*, said in a recent e-mail communication to me [3]:

> I would say that a configuration management tool is a real "must have." There is going to be lots of confusion among the pieces of the project and the manager and the team needs a way to establish and track versions of the system as they move toward completion, termination or whatever.

- There is an obvious benefit to having the CM tools well-integrated with the other primary development tools. Thus, Microsoft's Source-Safe may or may not be the best version-control software, but the fact that it's well-integrated with Visual Basic is a big argument in its favor. Similarly, many other development tools are integrated with InterSolv's PVCS, IBM's ENVY/Developer, or other comparable CM tools.

- *Testing, debugging tools*—many of us would automatically include these tools with the "basic" development tools that allow us to create code, compile it, and run it. But, as we moved from mainframe on-line applications to GUI-oriented client-server systems, we gradually realized that an entirely new set of testing tools were not only appropriate, but often essential; and, tools from vendors like SQA and Mercury Interactive still aren't widely enough distributed in the organizations I visit. Similarly, project teams moving into the world of the Internet and Web-based applications probably need a whole new set of testing and debugging tools.

- *Project management (estimating, scheduling, PERT/GANTT, etc.)*—there's a tendency to think of these as the "manager's toolkit," and that may be the case; perhaps it's only the project manager that needs to recompute the project's "critical path" on a daily basis. But, in this same category, I would include estimating tools like ESTI-MACS (developed by Howard Rubin, and available from Computer Associates), CHECKPOINT (from Software Productivity Research), and SLIM (from Quantitative Software Management). These are essential tools, in my opinion, because they support the dynamic re-evaluation of schedules and deadlines throughout the project.

- *Toolkit of reusable components*—if the project team is familiar with the concept of software reuse, and if it regards reuse as a strategic weapon with which to accomplish high levels of productivity, a toolkit of reusable components needs to be on the list of "must-have" tools. This might be a collection of VBX components for Visual Basic, the ParcPlace-Digitalk Smalltalk class library, or Microsoft's MFC class library for C++; obviously, it could also include some in-house components developed by other project teams within the organization. The choice is usually language-dependent, and it's another one of those areas that needs to be used consistently by everyone within the project team.

- *CASE tools for analysis/design*—some project teams regard CASE tools as a "crutch" for novice developers, but others consider them as essential as word processors. My preference is for the CASE tool that's simple, inexpensive, and flexible; aside from that, I won't recommend any particular product or vendor, because the real answer to the question of which CASE tool to use is, "it depends..." Indeed, as Doug Scott suggested in a recent e-mail message [4] to me, it might not require any technology at all:

> The best device is a large diagram pinned to the wall. It might contain the (partially complete) E/R diagrams for the system, or the process flows, or whatever. But it gives people a focus for discussing the design, and it costs next to nothing.

As I'll discuss below, the biggest problem with CASE tools is that they encourage (and sometimes enforce) a methodology that the project team doesn't understand and doesn't particularly want to use.

6.2 TOOLS AND PROCESS

The issue of CASE tools, mentioned above, is probably the most obvious example of a truism: tools and processes are inextricably linked together. There's no point in using a structured analysis CASE tool if you've never heard of the acronyms DFD and ERD. Such a CASE tool is not only useless, but an incredible burden, if the project team sincerely believes that ERDs and DFDs are meaningless forms of bureaucratic documentation produced solely to get the Methodology Police off their backs.

The situation is not always so black-and-white. For example, the project team might feel that data flow diagrams are useful, but only as an "informal" modeling tool. Thus, a "flexible" CASE tool might be considered a benefit, while a "hard-line" CASE tool would be rejected. Consider the obvious analogy with a word processor: We all appreciate the benefits of the spell-checker, but we don't want to be forced to use it, and it's quite likely that we *never* use the grammar-checker because it's too slow and clumsy (at least, that's *my* excuse for not using it on Microsoft Word!). We would be even more annoyed if the word processor steadfastly refused to allow the word "ain't" within a document, or required that any phrases considered racist or sexist be approved in advance by the Political Correctness Committee. A few more "features" like that would be enough to make us all go back to paper and pencil.

What this means, of course, is that the death march project team must *first* agree on the processes and methodologies it intends to follow, and it must decide which of those processes are going to be followed religiously—and which ones will be honored in spirit, but perhaps not to the letter of the law. Once this has been decided, the tools and technology can be chosen—or rejected!—accordingly. In this same fashion, the project manager may decide to adopt a particular tool to enforce a process that everyone agrees on intellectually, but is likely to practice in a sloppy fashion; two good examples are version control and configuration management.

One of the biggest myths about software tools in *any* software project—and a particular danger in a death march project—is that the tool will be a "silver bullet" that will somehow accomplish miracles. Miracles, of course, is what senior management is looking for; and even the project manager may be tempted by the vendors' advertising claims that programming, testing, or various other activities will be improved by a factor of ten through the genius of their tools.

Aside from the problem that such tools are usually brand-new and that nobody knows how to use them (which I'll discuss below), there's a more fundamental point to consider: The only way such a tool *could* be a silver bullet is if it allows or forces the developers to change their process. For example, if I write a program and then compile it, I do so according to a particular process. Perhaps I conduct a peer-level walkthrough before the compilation, or perhaps I precede the programming activity with a formal, detailed design process. Now, if you give me a compiler that's ten percent faster than the one I've been using, I'll be happier and somewhat more efficient; maybe the productivity of the overall project will increase by some incremental amount. *But I won't change my process.*

On the other hand, if you give me a compiler that's ten times faster, then it *will* change my process. That's what happened when we went from batch-mode, overnight compiles to on-line compilation in the 1970s, and then compilation on one's own PC/workstation in the 1980s, and then various combinations of incremental compiling (á la Delphi) and interpretive execution (á la Visual Basic). Because of this, many developers have eliminated detailed design prior to coding, on the theory that they can compose programs extemporaneously; the practice of walkthroughs has also been eliminated in many projects, on the assumption that the programmer can find and change his or her own defects efficiently.

Hardly anyone objects to the prospect of using improved technology that permits the *elimination* of processes that were considered boring and tedious. But, it's more difficult to introduce new technology that requires us to *add* processes, or *modify* processes that we were comfortable with. A good example is the process of reuse and the associated technology of reuse libraries, browsers, and related tools. The project teams that use this technology can effectively raise their level of reuse from approximately 20 percent (a level that I call "accidental" or "ad hoc" reuse) to 60 percent or more; indeed, if the technology is matched with a corporate-wide reuse process, the level of reuse can reach 80-90 percent or more.

The difference between a 20 percent level of reuse and an 80 percent level of reuse is equivalent to a four-fold improvement in productivity. And, as Paul Bassett points out in a new book on reuse [2], the subsequent incremental increases in reuse have more profound benefits than you might think. If the level of reuse rises from 80 percent to 90 percent, it means that instead of having to develop 20 percent of the code "from scratch," the project team only has to develop 10 percent. Thus, their workload has effectively been cut in half.

This is all very exciting—indeed, worthy of being called a "silver bullet"—but it's utterly irrelevant if the project team (and ultimately the entire organization) is unable or unwilling to change its software processes with regard to reuse. The irony is that most organizations will blame their failures on the technology itself: They'll buy an expensive class library, or they'll replace their old software development methodology with object-oriented techniques on the theory that objects are synonymous with reuse; and, when they eventually find they've achieved no measurable increase in reuse, they'll blame the problem on objects, or on the vendor of the class library, or on whatever other technology they've depended on. Meanwhile, the process is exactly the same as it was before. The culture of the organization is expressed with the following phrase: "Only wimps reuse other people's code; *real* programmers write their own damn code!"

From the perspective of a death march project, there's a very simple moral here: If the introduction of new tools *requires* the team's "standard" process to be changed dramatically, then it will add significantly to the project risk and probably contribute to the failure of the project. This sometimes gets muddled with the issues of training and of learning the mechanics of how to operate the tools (I'll discuss that below). But, the more fundamental problem is usually that of changing behavior, which is what software processes are all about. It's hard enough to do under normal circumstances, when we feel that we have lots of time and a supportive environment to slowly become comfortable with the new process. And for obvious reasons, it's usually a disaster in a death march project, when we don't have enough time, and we don't have a supportive environment.

6.3 THE RISKS OF CHOOSING NEW TOOLS

As noted above, some death march projects grab onto new tools and technology as a silver bullet to achieve far higher levels of productivity than would otherwise be possible. Let's assume for the moment that we've found some way to solve the cultural and political problems of process change that were discussed above. What else do we have to worry about?

The two most likely risks are technology and training. In many cases, the silver bullet tool is so new that it's not even available in a commercial form; usually, someone on the project team downloads the beta version from the Internet. Or, the tool can't be integrated with any of the other tools used by the project team; the vendor has made vague promises, but in the meantime, the tool's import-export capability is riddled with bugs. Or, the tool isn't supported—it was developed by a graduate student in Uzbekistan, or (even worse!) it was developed in-house by one of the software developers who sees nothing strange about the idea of a bank developing its own CASE tool or an insurance company developing its own DBMS.

Let's assume for the moment that the tool is solid, reliable, and available from a reputable vendor that provides top-notch support. In that case, the problem is likely to be one of training—for if the tool was already being widely used throughout the organization, nobody would have characterized it as a "silver bullet" that would miraculously save the death march team from certain disaster. Occasionally, you'll find a death march project team that begs for permission to use a powerful tool its members have all used in a previous job—but this is rare indeed. In most cases, neither the project team members nor anyone else in the organization has ever seen or used the tool before.

As mentioned before, any non-trivial tool usually has strong implications about the corresponding software process; thus, a new tool often implies a new process. Though such a correspondence should be obvious, it's remarkable how often the vendor's training representative gets half-way through a five-day workshop on how to operate the tool before finding that the students (whose managers are already panicked about falling five days behind schedule as a consequence of attending the workshop!) have absolutely no understanding of the process supported by the tool. It's awfully demoralizing, for example, to spend two days showing a reluctant student how to draw an ERD and then have him or her ask, "By the way, what *is* an entity? And since I'm gonna program everything in C++, why should I care about all of this stuff?"

But, let's assume that the project team members understand the process supported (and automated) by the tool, and that they have enthusiastically agreed that they will carry out the practice in their project; from 20 years of experience teaching structured and object-oriented methods, I know that this is a naive assumption, but there's no point in going further unless we do. So, *if* we assume that there are no technical problems with the tool, and *if* we assume that the corresponding software processes won't cause a problem, *then* all that is left is the training and practice associated with the tool itself.

How long does this take? Obviously, it depends on the nature and complexity of the tool—as well as its user interface, its on-line help features, and assorted other issues. In the best case, the developers will be able to figure out how to use the tool without any formal training at all; that's what the project manager and various other managers outside the project desperately want to believe, for they regard *any* training as a waste of time, and a distraction from the "real work" of the project. But, the more realistic estimate is that it will take an hour, a day, or a week to learn how to use the tool. Whether that takes the form of a classroom session, or reading a book, or just "playing" with the tool, it still takes time.

And, the training activity does *not* provide a thoroughly trained, infinitely experienced user of the tool. Training is not a binary phenomenon: The project team members don't go from a state of utter ignorance to a state of sublime mastery of the tool at the end of a one-week training class. This should be obvious, but it somehow baffles senior management, which tends to grumble and complain, "Okay, we spent all that money for those high-priced trainers, and we wasted all that time in the classroom when those lazy, good-for-nothin' programmers could have been coding. Now I want to see some *real* productivity with that silver bullet tool you talked us into getting for them!" Perhaps it's not so surprising that senior management would be so naive, since they wouldn't know a software tool if they fell over one; but sadly, I've seen the same reaction from many technically-oriented death march project managers.

In a wonderful article [5], my colleague Meilir Page-Jones argues that there are seven stages of mastery in software engineering; his article focuses on *methodologies*, but I believe that it applies equally well to tools and technology. In the list below, I've added my own estimates for how long it would take the average software developer to reach various stages, assuming that the tool or technology was of average sophistication and complexity:

1. *Innocent* (has never heard of Technology X)—this obviously requires no time at all.
2. *Aware* (has read an article about Technology X)—roughly an hour, in most cases, is enough for a software developer to be in a position where he or she can voice strong opinions about the advantages and disadvantages of the tool, even though he or she has never seen or used it.
3. *Apprentice* (has attended a five-day workshop)—a week, perhaps compressed into two days because of the pressure of a death march project. But, note that at this point, the developer has probably done nothing more than play with canned tutorials provided by the vendor, or dabbled with a small exercise to illustrate the features of the tool. He or she hasn't encountered the glitches, shortcomings, and "gotchas" of the tool; he or she hasn't seen how (or if) it will scale up for large, complex projects; he or she hasn't tried to integrate it with most of the other tools in the environment.
4. *Practitioner* (ready to use Technology X on a real project)—a month is probably required to explore the nuances of the tool and become sufficiently comfortable to use the tool on a "real" project.
5. *Journeyman* (uses Technology X naturally on the job; complains bitterly if it is taken away)—this usually takes 6–12 months, and if the tool really is a silver bullet, the developer becomes an evangelist, doing his or her best to persuade everyone that it's the most wonderful tool on earth.
6. *Master* (has internalized the details of Technology X; knows when to break the rules)—usually two to three years, which also means that the developer has survived through two or three new product releases, has found all of the support groups and discussion groups on the Internet, and knows all of the unlisted phone numbers for the technical support gurus at the vendor's organization.
7. *Expert* (writes books, gives lectures at conferences, looks for ways to extend Technology X into new galaxies)—Page-Jones was focusing on methodologies in his paper, and it's not clear that this applies to tools and technology.

TABLE 6.1 PAGE-JONES' SEVEN STAGES OF SOFTWARE ENGINEERING MASTERY

6.4 SUMMARY

Does the gloomy discussion in this chapter mean that we should use no tools at all? Are we supposed to abandon all technology and resort to old-fashioned keypunch machines? Should we assume that technology can *never* save us?

The rhetorical nature of these questions is intended to remind you that common sense should prevail in all such discussions. When the stars and planets align themselves just *so*, maybe technology *will* save us, at least on one or two death march projects. And we should certainly take advantage of as much advanced technology as we can, because it can leverage our intellectual efforts, and relieve us of time-consuming, error-prone tedious tasks associated with software development.

In the best of all worlds, the software developers will have had a chance to learn, experiment, and practice with high-powered tools in a less-risky environment; indeed, in the best case, advanced tools have already been deployed throughout the organization, and are part of the culture and infrastructure of the organization. And in this case, we wouldn't need to have any discussion about tools and technology at all; we would simply pick up our tools and go to work on the death march project.

The reason for the discussion in this chapter—and the reason all of this *is* relevant in most death march projects—is that the organization is using mediocre tools, *or* someone believes that a completely new form of technology, just announced breathlessly by a start-up vendor last week, will somehow save the day. The former scenario is depressing, but all too common; and the latter scenario is also common, for the simple reason that technology advances quickly and relentlessly in our field.

If new technology could be introduced without any impact on our software processes, and if it didn't require training and practice on the part of the developers, then we would be faced with a simple cost-benefit decision. And, since the natural instinct of many higher-level managers is to assume that a problem can be eliminated by simply throwing money at it, I find that there tends to be far more brand-new technology used on death march projects than on normal projects. The irony, as I've tried to explain in this chapter, is that the new tool can be the straw that breaks the camel's back; thus, project failure is blamed on the tool. As Sharon Marsh Roberts put it [6]:

> When the team is required to think clearly more than 60 hours per week, it's a bad time to invoke complex logic. Anything that requires a new mode of effort or a more sophisticated way of thinking is a problem.
>
> Doing something new requires the flexibility to "get it wrong" on the first iteration without becoming desperate.

So, use whatever tools make sense for your death march project, regardless of whether the rest of the world thinks they are advanced or old-fashioned. And remember that if you *do* use new tools, it's going to have an impact on the people and processes within the death march project. As Thoreau put it so eloquently 150 years ago:

> But lo! men have become the tools of their tools.
>
> Henry David Thoreau, *Walden*, "Economy" (1854).

Notes

1. When this book was being written in the summer of 1996, there were grave concerns that *exactly* this phenomenon would prevent many U.S. government agencies from finishing the biggest death march project of all time by the non-negotiable deadline. I'm talking, of course, about the Year-2000 project.

2. Sometimes the politics can get pretty nasty here. During the past year, I've observed a number of forlorn IBM employees using Lotus Freelance instead of PowerPoint and Lotus 1-2-3 instead of Excel, because it wasn't worth the political battles they would have faced otherwise. Similarly, I'm not sure I would want to be part of a project team at Microsoft that decided, circa August 1996, to use Netscape Navigator rather than Internet Explorer.

3. Ed,
```
Ch 6 comments follow -
1. If your team had only ONE kind of "optional" or "discretionary"
tool/technology to support them in a death march project, what
would it be? My assumption here is that every project has an
absolute bare-minimum of required things like compilers and
debuggers, but there's an awful lot that (a) the project team may
```

not have immediately available, (b) senior management would perceive the acquisition of such new technology as expensive, and (c) one or more managers or kibitzers on the sidelines would say "oh, you don't need THAT tool!".

I would say that a configuration management tool is a real "must have." There is going to be lots of confusion among the pieces of the project and the manager and the team needs a way to establish and track versions of the system as they move toward completion, termination or whatever.

2. How important are CASE tools for death march projects? In this context, I mean what we used to call "upper-CASE" tools that support analysis and design-level stuff; depending on how much money you spend, they might also generate code, wash the dishes, and provide various other useful services.

I find them very useful - at the same level as word processors. They allow the team to communicate using a standard format. I've found that inexpensive CASE tools work just fine.

3. How important are "visual" development environments in death march projects? I don't want to be language-specific here, since there are visual versions of most of the high-level programming languages available today. But the issue here is using a "drag-and-drop" kind of development tool for building programs, versus the older style of text editors to type in lines of code, followed by compile, link, test, etc.?

In the situations where I have seen these used, I've been impressed.

They appear to remove a lot of the "housekeeping" that takes programmer and analyst time. I have yet to lead a project that uses these tools, but I'm hopeful.

4. How important do you think "groupware" tools are? I don't want to be too specific here, since everyone has a slightly different definition -- but I'm thinking of tools similar to Lotus Notes for organizing "threads" of discussions and fostering collaboration, coordination, and communication. I would be interested to know if anyone has used more exotic forms of groupware; if you want to see examples, read Michael Schrage's book "No More Teams!". (And if you've never heard of the book, take a look at my review of his book, which I've posted in the "articles" section of my Web site at http://www.yourdon.com)

E-Mail is critical and document and code libraries are a "must," but the benefits of other groupware functionality might be harder to identify. In a crunch-mode environment, face-to-face working has a lot to recommend it.

5. Are there any tools, or technology-approach, that you consider highly risky or dangerous for death-march projects? If you had to advise a death march project manager to AVOID a particular tool or technology, what would it be?

The standard rules apply here. You don't pick a technology that is inappropriate for the task at hand. Using OO and the Web as building blocks for a telephone company's billing system might sound sexy, but the nature of the job is batch processing and you might be better off with COBOL.

Hope this helps,

--JB

4. Ed,

> 1. If your team had only ONE kind of "optional" or "discretionary"
> tool/technology to support them in a death march project, what
> would it be?

I'd get a CASE tool which could enable requirements through to module/object definition. Code generation is not IMHO a real problem, but taking requirements through to low-level models is. And yes, we still have those who think you can just sit down and write an OLTP system in assembler.

Failing the CASE tool, then an integrated set of tools such as Smartsuite or Office, so that we could come up with something similar cheaply and quickly. And we need the spreadsheet.

HOWEVER. The best device is a large diagram pinned to the wall. It might contain the (partially complete) E/R diagrams for the system, or the process flows, or whatever. But it gives people a focus for discussing the design, and it costs next to nothing.

> 2. How important are CASE tools for death march projects?

Important, if introduced with appropriate training at the beginning of the project. A disaster if not.

> 3. How important are "visual" development environments in
> death march projects?

I'm beginning to accept that the "visual" revolution is to do with right- and left-brainedness, and since programmers are supposed to be left-brained (or is it right?) they would be quite happy with command line tools. Analysts, however, and designers, need to be able to visualise things, and if the tool gives the ability to do that (some do, but the resultant diagrams simply don't help) then they're useful.

Tha wall chart (see above) does help, though.

> 5. Are there any tools, or technology-approach, that you consider
> highly risky or dangerous for death march projects

Most project management tools are, IMHO, a load of rubbish. PERT
is enough to find the critical path, but many tools insist that
you do full resource allocation before the project even starts. I
use a spreadsheet, but I'd love a copy of an old-fashioned PERT
diagrammer where I could add resources during the project (which
is when I find out what I'm getting) rather than months before.
--Doug

5. Meilir Page-Jones, "The Seven Stages in Software Engineering," *American Programmer*, July-August 1990.

6. Ed,
>> 1. If your team had only ONE kind of "optional" or
"discretionary" tool/technology to support them in a death march
project, what would it be? My assumption here is that every project
has an absolute bare-minimum of required things like compilers and
debuggers, but there's an awful lot that (a) the project team may
not have immediately available, (b) senior management would
perceive the acquisition of such new technology as expensive, and
(c) one or more managers or kibitzers on the sidelines would say
"oh, you don't need THAT tool!".<<
I'd choose Infomodeler or something similar. Inexpensive tool
which functions to do some elementary things. Feature it, for the
CASE-weary, as a drawing tool, so that we can communicate with the
users.
>>2. How important are CASE tools for death march projects? In this
context, I mean what we used to call "upper-CASE" tools that
support analysis and design-level stuff; depending on how much
money you spend, they might also generate code, wash the dishes,
and provide various other useful services.<<
Pick one that supports high-level design and communications. If
it happens to also generate code, fine. If not, that's OK. Just
don't pick something that does the dishes, because it will be too
hard to learn and too easy to blame for design delays.
>>3. How important are "visual" development environments in death
march projects? I don't want to be language-specific here, since
there are visual versions of most of the high-level programming
languages available today. But the issue here is using a "drag-
and-drop" kind of development tool for building programs, versus
the older style of text editors to type in lines of code, followed
by compile, link, test, etc?<<
If it works for the programming team, it's important. If the team
is accustomed to text-edited COBOL code, who am I to complain?

At this point there are plenty of experienced VB programmers, for example.

>>4. How important do you think "groupware" tools are? I don't want to be too specific here, since everyone has a slightly different definition -- but I'm thinking of tools similar to Lotus Notes for organizing "threads" of discussions and fostering collaboration, coordination, and communication. I would be interested to know if anyone has used more exotic forms of groupware; if you want to see examples, read Michael Schrage's book "No More Teams!". (And if you've never heard of the book, take a look at my review of his book, which I've posted in the "articles" section of my Web site at http://www.yourdon.com) <<

I'll go see your Web site and the review. "I'll be back."

>>5. Are there any tools, or technology-approach, that you consider highly risky or dangerous for death march projects? If you had to advise a death march project manager to AVOID a particular tool or technology, what would it be? <<

Pick one of the following, depending upon prior experience of the team:

a. C or C++

b. Smalltalk

c. AI

d. any new full-lifecycle CASE tool

e. UNIX or any other operating system that's new for the team

When the team is required to think clearly more than 60 hours per week, it's a bad time to invoke complex logic. Anything that requires a new mode of effort or a more sophisticated way of thinking is a problem.

Doing something new requires the flexibility to "get it wrong" on the first iteration without becoming desperate.

--Sharon

Additional References

Michael Schrage, *No More Teams! Mastering the Dynamics of Creative Collaboration* (New York: Doubleday-Dell Publishing Company, 1995).

Paul G. Bassett, *Framing Software Reuse: Lessons from the Real World* (Upper Saddle River, NJ: Prentice Hall, 1996). ISBN 0-13-327859-X.

DEATH MARCH AS A WAY OF LIFE

Culture is a sham if it is only a sort of Gothic front put on an iron building—like Tower Bridge—or a classical front put on a steel frame—like the *Daily Telegraph* building in Fleet Street. Culture, if it is to be a real thing and a holy thing, must be the product of what we actually do for a living—not something added, like sugar on a pill.

Eric Gill, *Essays,* **"Education for What"** (1948)

Throughout this book, I've perpetuated a contradiction which we now need to confront. On the one hand, I've argued that death march projects are qualitatively different from all of the other "normal" projects that take place within a software development organization. On the other hand, I suggested in Chapter 1 that the circumstances leading to death march projects—schedules and budgets 50-100 percent more ambitious than normal, functionality requests 50-100 percent more advanced than normal—occur more and frequently in today's organizations.

Many developers and managers might ask whether it's rational to *plan* on having death march projects. As John Boddie [1], author of *Crunch Mode*, points out about the industry in which he has worked:

> I spent years in the lottery business, where everything is in crunch mode because that is the way that the industry grew up. If you don't want to work in this fashion, you can't play in this sandbox. Developers in this industry put up with it because they have tasted success in short, high-intensity projects and have been given considerable freedom to do things like take two months off between projects. The teams consider themselves to be elite and the companies in this business treat them that way.

And, as Doug Scott suggests [2],

> Management have different drivers. They know that the risk of outsourcing their empires is higher now than it's ever been, and want to deliver. They also know that we take an awfully long time to deliver because there are all sorts of bureaucratic time-wasting procedures in place. They think that, if they stress the importance of this particular project over all others, these procedures will be trimmed without them having to do anything specific about it. They accept that they can't put the best people on the job, and they accept that better technology might help if it weren't for the long learning curve which prohibits the use of new technology on this project, so they can't use it. Or alternatively, they believe industry hype and think that the new technology will magically be mature, error-free, and instantly understandable to all concerned.

But, if death march projects are the norm, then should we even call them "death march"? Doesn't it just become part of the overall corporate culture? I'll begin by discussing why such a transformation might take place within a rational software organization, and then move on to the more significant question of: How can we *change* the culture of today's traditional organization so that it can effectively support death march projects without making them seem like such an anomaly?

7.1 WHY WOULD DEATH MARCH PROJECTS BECOME THE NORM?

Let's begin by reviewing the likelihood of death march projects becoming the norm. I've suggested throughout this book that there are at least three reasons this could occur:

- *The organization is in the midst of ongoing crises*—this might be the result of an unfortunate coincidence of several unexpected crises occurring within a short period of time; but, it's more commonly associated with organizations that are in serious trouble, desperately trying to cope with a "sea of change" in the marketplace, or with the technology that people are using. In most cases, such an organization is in far too desperate a position to be able to step back and reorganize itself to carry on all of its projects in a planned, rational fashion that achieves the dramatic improvements associated with death march projects. The rare exception is when a "turn-around" senior manager is brought in to lead the company out of crisis; the new manager might adopt an entirely different way of doing things.

- *Management/customers have adopted the approach as their standard negotiating position*—as noted in Chapters 1 and 2, this is often how the first death march project begins; but if it works once, why not do it again? If the marketing department, or the finance department, or some other part of the organization is faced with the need for a "permanent" reengineering to achieve a competitive level of productivity and profitability, that might also include a permanent decision to insist that all of the vendors and suppliers with whom it interacts reengineer themselves in a similar way. From the perspective of these internal corporate departments, the IS/IT department is just another "supplier" of goods and services. A variation of this is the edict from senior management to the IS/IT department:

"Unless you people radically improve your productivity on *all* your projects, we're going to outsource the whole thing to India!"

- *It's part of the company's "strategic advantage"*—this appears to be the case with organizations like EDS, and it's the explicit approach of organizations like Cambridge Technology Partners. It makes sense for a software consulting organization, where the performance of software project teams *is* the business. But, we could easily imagine the same thing in other "information-rich" businesses like banking, insurance, and telecommunications—where the ability to deliver new software-based "products" to the marketplace depends largely on how quickly the software can be developed. To the extent that this is true, I expect to see more and more organizations adopting an overall death march culture.

Whether this makes sense for an organization is one thing; whether it makes sense for the individual software developers and project managers is likely to be something else indeed. The organization's perspective is obviously important, but I want to focus on the perspective of the individual and project manager here; after all, I don't expect many CEOs and marketing VPs to read this book.

The key question for the software developer and project manager is: Having survived one death march project, would you be willing to do it again? The answer to this question depends largely, as you might imagine, on whether the first project succeeded. After all, if you've just finished a suicide- or ugly-style project, you're likely to be physically and emotionally exhausted. Your ego and sense of self-worth have been shattered, and your personal life may be in shambles. Who on earth would want to do it again? Even the so-called kamikaze projects, where you sacrificed your own personal needs for a glorious (but losing) corporate cause, must be recognized, at the end, as failures. You may feel that it was a noble sacrifice, but unless you have the personality of a martyr, it's not likely that you would volunteer to repeat the experience.

Note that the "ugly-style" project, as I described it in Chapter 1, may have succeeded; thus, senior management and the end users may be thrilled. And the project manager may be thrilled too, especially if he or she reaped a huge reward of some kind at the end of the project. If you're one of the surviving team members, you may or may not be thrilled with the results; the fact that there's a lot of blood on the floor, and that numerous lives and careers may have been wasted, might not bother you at all. Indeed, it becomes part of the culture—part of the thrill is associated with the fact that there *is* a lot of blood on the floor.

Obviously, the kind of project where the chances are greatest of finding volunteers for a repeat performance is the mission impossible project: the project that not only succeeded, but left everyone feeling really proud of the miracle they performed. If there is time for a project post-mortem, it's crucial to ask at this point: "What made it possible for us to succeed?" Was it only luck? Was it entirely due to the charisma of the project manager, or the genius of the database designer, or the fact that the end user and systems analyst fell madly in love and got married at the end of the project? The underlying question is: Is there any rational reason to expect that we could pull off such a stunt again?

It's important to ask these questions as early as possible, because the organization is likely to repeat the experience whether or not the individuals think it's a good idea. As noted above, in the extreme case, the organization does so because it must; some organizations take a long time to die, and the last five to ten years might be nothing but an endless succession of death marches. Even in less extreme cases, the failure of one death march project is not necessarily enough to make the organization abandon its approach; as noted in previous chapters, the failure is often blamed on the project manager or the silver bullet technology. "Next time," the CEO vows, "we won't make those mistakes again; we'll have a new project manager and a new silver bullet technology."

Obviously, if the first death march project succeeded, there's a much higher chance that the end users and senior management will try to do it again; but, this may be the point where the project team individuals decide to say "Sayonara," form a conga line, and dance right out the door. There's not much point using this action as a threat; management generally believes—rightly or wrongly—that fresh new volunteers can be obtained. The best thing for the exhausted death march survivors to do is wish everyone well, and go look for a calmer, saner existence somewhere else.

7.2 ESTABLISHING A DEATH MARCH "CULTURE"

Let's assume that the organization *has* decided to change its culture and begin carrying out all of its projects in a death march style. As noted above, this might happen without any conscious decision, and it might happen whether or not the individuals are willing to tolerate more than a single death march project. But, let's assume that it's a *conscious* strategy on the part of IS/IT management, or senior managers above the IS/IT department. What are the consequences, and how can a typical organization bring about such a change?

The most important thing that must happen is the replacement of the "normal" culture for developing software with the "radical" culture embodied by the death march project. This change won't happen quickly or easily, for much of the bureaucracy will argue strenuously for the continuation of the older approaches. But, the savvy organization will acknowledge that if the first death march project succeeds, the success will be largely a matter of luck and stubbornness on the part of the team. If the organization wants subsequent death march projects to succeed with any predictability, it must change.

The changes will affect the tools and technologies, the processes and methodologies, the management styles, and the planning and scheduling strategies used by the IS/IT organization. It will involve issues like these:

- What kind of people should the organization hire? Within the legal and ethical constraints of non-discrimination policies, chances are that the organization will be looking for younger, more energetic people, and it may even show a preference for unmarried people, and people with few outside interests. Young, unmarried, antisocial, workaholic techno-nerds are just what many organizations need for their death march projects.

- What should prospective new employees be told about the organization? It seems to me not only unethical, but downright stupid, to hide the fact that the organization intends to pursue a death march strategy on its projects. Indeed, the organizations that do adopt this approach are usually quite proud of it, just as organizations are proud of any other aspect of their culture. The organization may not want to point out that only a small percentage of incoming recruits will survive the first death march project (just as colleges often don't want to admit that they flunk out a large percentage of the incoming freshman class), but it *should* point out that it expects more than a 9-to-5 workday.

- What impact should death march projects have on formal career advance policies—e.g., promotions, raises, and bonuses? It's relatively common in law firms and Big-6 accounting firms, for example, to tell incoming recruits that they should expect a period of seven to nine years to elapse before they become partners; there may be intermediate steps of "manager" and "senior manager," but nobody has any illusions that the long hours and hard work are going to disappear after the first year or two.

- What impact should death march projects have on the style of management? Should managers be *expected* to "burn out" their team members and discard them at the beginning of their project? Or, does the project manager have the added responsibility of making the team members feel good about themselves, as well as delivering a successful system to the end users? Note that if a rational organization decides to adopt a death march culture (as opposed to having a series of such projects forced upon it), it presumably wants those projects to succeed; in the vocabulary of Chapter 1, this means that the projects will be "mission impossible" or "ugly" as a matter of conscious, corporate choice. But, if things *are* going to be ugly, and if people are going to be burned up and thrown away at the end of a project, why not use consultants? Sharon Marsh Roberts puts it this way [3]:

> I believe the organization needs to find ways of renewing resources. One alternative is to use many consultants, who are expected to buy into the "earn lots of money and get out of here" workstyle. Another is to have a "safe haven" (maintenance assignments) where employees can be transferred between death marches.

- What kinds of tools should the organization equip itself with if *every* project is going to be a death march project? If it appears that a major factor in the success of the first death march project was a reusable class library of objects, or a RAD-oriented visual programming tool, then perhaps every project should have it.

- What kind of infrastructure does the organization need to support death march projects? This might involve company-wide e-mail or a more elaborate groupware infrastructure based on Lotus Notes. But, it could also involve significant changes in the human infrastructure—i.e., the network of administrators and support staff that perhaps needs to be augmented, and the layers of bureaucracy that need to be pruned.

- What kind of processes are appropriate for a death march culture? Triage, formal vs. informal processes, and many of the other issues discussed in Chapter 5 need to be addressed at the organizational level, so that each team will get the kind of support that it needs when it attempts to implement and practice death march processes. Note also that processes are subtly influenced by the *length* of a project; most organizations find that death march projects are more likely to succeed if they're kept short. As Bill Hamaker puts it [4],

> Do it as lots of small death marches rather than a few big ones. Concentrate on creating an organization that can learn from the systems that resulted from the death marches. In particular have adequate "non-project" time for staff to evaluate what's good and bad about the systems, maybe use this time as a way for staff to rest between death marches.

7.3 DEATH MARCH TRAINING

In Chapters 6 and 7, I discussed the issue of training for a death march project team being exposed to new processes and tools. But, the need for such training changes if death march projects become part of the corporate culture. In these cases, the appropriate processes and tools should be part of the "standard" approach, which eliminates the need for introducing them as something new and radical at the beginning of each project.

Realistically, though, there will be a transition period while the organization shifts its mode of operation from the older form of projects to the newer style. But even during the transition period, the ideal situation would be to shift the required training out of the death march project environment and into the normal environment; indeed, such training should be considered part of the transition process. With any luck, this will enable the training to be carried out in a more orderly basis, without the time pressures that are normally a factor when the training occurs in the midst of a death march project.

Appropriate training must also be provided for new people hired into the organization. Novices—e.g., new college graduates who have never had a full-time software development job—don't have to be told that the new approach is different from the old approach; indeed, they don't even have to hear the term "death march." But they do need to be given the appropriate training in the methods, processes, and tools that the organization has found effective in death march projects. This is likely to be quite different from the older-style processes and tools that such recruits previously had to endure. (The irony is that as soon as the former recruits moved into their first project, they were often told by their project manager to ignore "all that classroom stuff" and adopt a more pragmatic attitude toward software development.) New recruits need to understand that the death march processes and tools are being adopted as a matter of proactive choice, rather than reactive desperation.

7.4 THE CONCEPT OF "WAR GAMES"

While these forms of training sound reasonable and rational, they're ignored in many smaller organizations; on-the-job training takes its place, and developers are expected to learn the processes and tools through some form of osmosis. It's even worse for managers—as my friend Tim Lister has remarked, the only training that most software project managers receive is the two words, "Good luck!"

Obviously, textbooks and classroom training on project management techniques, processes, and tools are important and helpful. But, many organizations feel that there's no substitute for the "real thing"—indeed, they consciously ignore classroom training, on the theory that once you've gone through a *real* death march project, you're a veteran in ways that you could never become through classroom exercises.

Rather than arguing whether the classroom is preferable to the "battlefield" of a death march project, I believe that organizations consider a compromise: a death march *simulator*. The analogy with "flight simulators" is more appropriate than you might think at first: Airline pilots use their simulators not only to practice normal takeoffs and landings, but for a wide variety of emergency situations they could not afford to carry out in a real airplane. And, flight simulators have the wonderful capability of letting you fly your airplane head-on into a mountain without killing anyone. Why not let a project manager, together with all of the members of the project team, fly their project into the equivalent of a mountain, so they can experience the problems without killing anyone? And, why not require both developers and managers to make an annual visit to the death march project simulator, just as airline pilots do?

Skeptics might argue that such a simulator would not replicate the pressure and tension that one experiences in a real project; airline pilots who have used their simulators to practice emergency situations would strenuously disagree. But, if we *really* need to simulate stress in a software project, we can borrow a familiar tactic from the military: war games. As DeMarco and Lister explain in their *Peopleware* book [5],

> War games help you to evaluate your relative strengths and weaknesses and help the organization to observe its global strengths and weaknesses.
>
> For the purpose of stimulative creative disorder, the most effective form of war game calls for participants to take part in teams.

Thus, a death march war game could consist of giving several different project teams the same "project scenario"—the same requirements, the same (compressed) amount of time, the same resources to work with. Or, if the death march culture still hasn't been standardized and formalized within the organization, tell each team that it can use whatever tools and processes it wants to—anything they can beg, borrow, or steal is fair game. The Australian Computer Society has been hosting such a war game at its annual conference since 1994, and several local consulting organizations now use it as part of their own training process.

To conduct a war game, or any other kind of "flight simulator" for death march projects, one needs to have a simulation model that can mimic the cause-and-effect consequences of various technical and managerial decisions in a project. I discussed this concept at length in my *Rise and Resurrection of the American Programmer*, and I've provided a list of references at the end of this chapter; of particular importance is Tarek Abdel-Hamid and Stuart E. Madnick's *Software Project Dynamics: An Integrated Approach* [6], which provides a complete, detailed simulation model of a medium-sized software project.

A simulation model can be implemented in virtually any programming language, but there are specialized languages and tools for such purposes. Of these, SIMSCRIPT, DYNAMO, and GPSS are perhaps the best known; the model described by Abdel-Hamid and Madnick is implemented in DYNAMO (and the entire program listing is published in the book's appendix). More recently, a number of "visual" modeling tools have appeared, most of them modestly priced. Of the commercial tools, the ones listed below are my favorites.

iThink (Macintosh, Windows)
High Performance Systems Inc., Hanover, NH
Phone: 603-643-9636, Fax: 603-643-9502

VenSim (Windows)
Ventana Systems, Belmont, MA
Phone: 617-489-5234, Fax: 617-489-5316

Professional DYNAMO (Windows)
Pugh-Robert Associates, Cambridge, MA
Phone: 617-864-8880, Fax: 617-864-8884

Extend (Macintosh and Windows)
Imagine That, Inc., San Jose, CA
Phone: 408-365-0305, Fax: 408-629-1251

Even with elegant tools and a wealth of published literature, there's no way of escaping the fact that it requires a serious investment and commitment to build a model that reflects a particular company's environment, and allows management to demonstrate the particular death march scenarios they feel important. Having been involved in several of these simulator projects and war game scenarios since the early 1990s, my experience is that it typically requires at least a few person-months of effort to have a realistic and well-tuned model; and as another illustration, it's interesting to note that the model published in *Software Project Dynamics: An Integrated Approach* [7] was Abdel-Hamid's Ph.D. thesis.

This means that such an effort is clearly beyond the ability of an individual project manager to develop as part of the training experience for a single death march project. It's clearly a corporate, strategic investment—and it may be more than a small, ten-person software company can afford to think about. But, for software organizations with hundreds, or even thousands, of people, it's a small investment indeed. Keep in mind the context in which all of this occurs: Management is looking for ways of institutionalizing processes and technology that will enable projects to *confidently* promise schedules, budgets, and deliverable functionality two or three times more ambitious than "normal" projects have experienced in the same environment. In planning for such a radical change, management is often prepared to spend vast sums of money—literally millions of dollars in some cases—to equip the developers with new workstations, visual programming tools, and object-oriented methodologies. To complain about the cost of a six-person-month effort to build a simulator is ludicrous; and to deny their project teams the experience of simulating a death march project before they risk millions of dollars on a *real* death march project is pig-headed.

Alas, senior management typically doesn't see it this way. They generally resent the time, effort, and cost of *any* training, and the cost and effort associated with death march simulators is seen as even less justifiable. This is one of the key reasons that a death march culture will never be successfully implemented in most large organizations.

7.5 SUMMARY

As noted throughout this book, death march projects have become inevitable in today's competitive and chaotic business environment. A few organizations have acknowledged this situation, and have begun planning for it in a rational manner. However, the history of the software industry for the past 40 years suggests that most of our organizations don't learn much from their past experiences, and are likely to regard each new death march project as a unique and novel experience. Even the organizations that realize death march projects are no longer isolated accidents will have a difficult time, for the established bureaucracy will continue to defend old standards, procedures, methodologies, and tools regardless of how inappropriate they may be.

One cheerful exception to this is the entrepreneurial start-up organization. By definition, such organizations have no prior culture to replace, and they are likely to regard death march projects as perfectly normal—after all, it's part of the mythos of start-up companies that everyone works insane hours while the company takes insane risks to compete against larger, established companies. And, if the fledgling company comes to the conclusion that its success is precisely *because* of this behavior, then it will probably try to institutionalize the behavior.

Of course, I'm speaking in generalities here, and there are lots of reasons why such an approach won't succeed. It's interesting, for example, that veteran software developers often bring much of their culture and work habits with them when they leave a large bureaucracy to start a new software venture. On the other hand, it seems just as common today as it was in the early days of my career for the younger generation of software developers to plunge into new projects on a work schedule that regards 18-hour days as "resting up" while the team gets ready for the *real* work. But, among the many things that *have* changed dramatically is the overall pace of work, which the folks at Netscape and Microsoft and numerous other organizations refer to simply as "Internet time." It's a concept that simply didn't exist for previous generations of software developers, and it's far more likely to lead to death march projects.

Regardless of whether the industry adopts death march projects as the norm, and regardless of whether your company manages such projects in a rational fashion, the fact remains that death march projects are carried out by individuals. I don't have a great deal of hope for the senior management and bureaucratic committees in most software organizations, but I do have a great deal of concern for the individuals who work the long nights and weekends on projects that are often doomed from the beginning. Bringing a death march project to a successful conclusion is obviously important, and I hope this book has provided some practical advice for doing just that; but *surviving* them is even more important! In the best of all worlds, our death march projects should deliver glorious results to the end user with a schedule and budget that will dazzle senior management, and we should do all of this with our health, our wits, our family, and our sense of humor firmly intact.

As E.B. White put it, perhaps in the midst of one of his own death march projects:

> I wake up each morning determined to change the World ... and also to have one hell of a good time.
>
> Sometimes that makes planning the day a little difficult.
>
> E.B. White

Notes

1. Ed,
Ch 7 query comments follow:
1. Does the concept make sense? Is there any rational reason why an organization would choose to make ALL of its software development projects death marches? Is there any rational reason why software developers would continue working in such an environment?
Ed, I spent years in the lottery business, where everything is in crunch mode because that is the way that the industry grew up. If you don't want to work in this fashion, you can't play in this sandbox. Developers in this industry put up with it because they have tasted success in short, high-intensity projects and have been given considerable freedom to do things like take two months off between projects. The teams consider themselves to be elite and the companies in this business treat them that way.
2. If it IS rational, how should the organization adapt itself to succeed? I'm particularly interested in "strategic" decisions that you could get the VP of Software, or the MIS Director, to support and pay for. Should all programmers be fitted with bulletproof vests? Should the organization scrap all of its existing tools and

buy a completely new set of "death march programming tools" for everyone on the staff?

Since the staffs are reasonably small, there is seldom a problem putting a lot of capital into each member of the team. A six-person team may have exclusive use of a dual-system configuration for testing and a third system for development. Team members will have a lot of power on their desks and there will seldom be a problem in finding money to try out something new that sounds promising. If you are a VP and know you have a twenty-person team to deal with, there are a lot of amenities you can consider that would make no sense if you had to direct 400 people.

3. The problem with most death march projects that I've seen is that nobody -- including the project manager! -- has any previous experience in such things. If it's going to be a "standard" way of organizing and carrying out projects within the organization, then what about the idea of a "flight simulator" (just like the airlines do for their pilots) for training fledgling death march project managers? I've run such things on an ad hoc basis in a couple of organizations, and I know that there are tools available (e.g., the iThink implementation of Tarek Abdel-Hamid's model of software projects). Has anyone seen this on a sustained basis, as part of standard corporate policy?

I haven't seen anything along the lines you mention. Death marches are sort of like a fraternity. You pledge and then you go through your initiation. Eventually, you may be named as Rush chairman and assigned to go get new members.

4. If you were a consultant, and you had 15 minutes to advise the VP of Software about what to do in order to make death march projects succeed on an on-going basis, what is the MOST important thing you would advise him/her to do?

Concentrate on getting the right people and finding ways to keep them sane.

5. Similarly, what's the most important thing you would advise him/her NOT to do?

Call in a nationally recognized consulting firm to re-engineer the software development process.

--JB

2. Ed,

Having been involved in death marches many times previously, and being faced with the start of a large project right now, I'd be really interested in what you find in Chapter 7.

> "death march projects as a way of life".
> 1. Does the concept make sense?

It has to, because it's pandemic (as you suggest). I think you've got a lot of the reasons from earlier threads.

Most of our estimates, we know, are only very approximate. I've been in the game a long time, and I know I won't get to within 50% of the real-time. But if there's time left over at the end of the project, it gets consumed in testing. So you know, within your bones, that time can be cut at the expense of quality. If the quality suffers, then they deserve it because they asked for a truncated job, so there's a blameless way of agreeing to a tight schedule.

Management have different drivers. They know that the risk of outsourcing their empires is higher now than it's ever been, and want to deliver. They also know that we take an awfully long time to deliver because there are all sorts of bureaucratic time-wasting procedures in place. They think that, if they stress the importance of this particular project over all others, these procedures will be trimmed without them having to do anything specific about it. They accept that they can't put the best people on the job, and they accept that better technology might help if it weren't for the long learning curve which prohibits the use of new technology on this project, so they can't use it. Or alternatively, they believe industry hype and think that the new technology will magically be mature, error-free, and instantly understandable to all concerned.

So the next project will be better, and it'll be done quicker, and it'll be done more cheaply. So you can pass that wonderful message back to the business - quicker and cheaper, and less to maintain. Who could object to that?

We are exactly in that situation. The guy who wants us to put it all on PCs and do away with the mainframe is the guy who's just come off a PC-based project which signally failed to deliver. But he knows what the problems are now (!)

> 2. If it IS rational, how should the organization adapt itself to
> succeed?

For me, it's small systems and small teams. Much architectural work up-front to split things right down to under 1000FP. But I can't tell you whether or not it works for me, because we haven't done it yet.

More later

Doug

3. Ed,

>> 1. Does the concept make sense? Is there any rational reason why an organization would choose to make ALL of its software

development projects death marches? Is there any rational reason why software developers would continue working in such an environment?<<

Perhaps. Perhaps the environment does not allow for consensus-building on a timely basis. By the time a business decision is reached, the system must be built. By the time a design is built to accommodate the business process, it's time to deliver the system that supports the process.

>>2. If it IS rational, how should the organization adapt itself to succeed? I'm particularly interested in "strategic" decisions that you could get the VP of Software, or the MIS Director, to support and pay for.<<

I believe the organization needs to find ways of renewing resources. One alternative is to use many consultants, who are expected to buy into the "earn lots of money and get out of here" workstyle. Another is to have a "safe haven" (maintenance assignments) where employees can be transferred between death marches.

>>Should all programmers be fitted with bulletproof vests? Should the organization scrap all of its existing tools and buy a completely new set of "death march programming tools" for everyone on the staff?<<

No weapons should be allowed in such environments. Clowns should be on site to deliver the joke of the day. Folks need to have ways of reducing frustration without creating more frustration for others.

And learning new tools is hardly apropos.

>>??3. The problem with most death march projects that I've seen is that nobody -- including the project manager! -- has any previous experience in such things. If it's going to be a "standard" way of organizing and carrying out projects within the organization, then what about the idea of a "flight simulator" (just like the airlines do for their pilots) for training fledgling death march project managers? I've run such things on an ad hoc basis in a couple of organizations, and I know that there are tools available (e.g., the iThink implementation of Tarek Abdel-Hamid's model of software projects). Has anyone seen this on a sustained basis, as part of standard corporate policy?<<

This is an interesting thought. However, I suspect that in most of the death marches I've seen (or observed from a distance) are a core of folks who are always asked to work with the project when it becomes most critical. Such folks never have been asked if this is the right way to proceed. Such folks have a tendency to tell

their peers, and perhaps even their bosses, how misspent the effort
is.

I know who those folks were in a project in which my husband was
involved.   I know who was always asked to "help" at critical
moments when I was in a corporate job. I suspect that I've worked
with some of the folks who filled that role on some consulting
assignments.

>>4. If you were a consultant, and you had 15 minutes to advise
the VP of Software about what to do in order to make death march
projects succeed on an on-going basis, what is the MOST important
thing you would advise him/her to do?<<

Build the teams and nurture the staff relationships. These folks
are required to grind away at the projects for most of their
working days. They are the ones who will either cooperate to make
a success or to make a failure.

>>5. Similarly, what's the most important thing you would advise
him/her NOT to do?<<

Don't lose touch with the users and their requirements.   They,
beyond all else, will determine the ultimate outcome.

Sharon

4. Ed,

>> 1. Does the concept make sense? Is there any rational reason
why an organization would choose to make ALL of its software
development projects death marches? Is there any rational reason
why software developers would continue working in such an
environment? <<

I doubt it. The only possible rational reason I can think of is
that the organization is not capable of controlling the IS group
in any other way.

>> 4. If you were a consultant, and you had 15 minutes to advise
the VP of Software about what to do in order to make death march
projects succeed on an on-going basis, what is the MOST important
thing you would advise him/her to do? <<

Do it as lots of small death marches rather than a few big ones.
Concentrate on creating an organization that can learn from the
systems that resulted from the death marches. In particular have
adequate "non-project" time for staff to evaluate what's good and
bad about the systems, maybe use this time as a way for staff to
rest between death marches.

--Bill

5. Tom DeMarco and Tim Lister, *Peopleware* (New York: Dorset House, 1987),
page 162.

6. Tarek Abdel-Hamid and Stuart E. Madnick, *Software Project Dynamics: An Integrated Approach* (Englewood Cliffs, NJ: Prentice-Hall, 1991).

7. See Note 6.

Additional References

Tarek Abdel-Hamid, "Organizational Learning: the key to software management Innovation," *American Programmer,* June 1991.

Tarek Abdel-Hamid and Stuart E. Madnick, "Impact of Schedule Estimation on Software Project Behavior," *IEEE Software,* May 1986.

Tarek Abdel-Hamid and S. E. Madnick, "Lessons Learned from Modeling the dynamics of software project management," *Comm. of the ACM* (December 1989).

Tarek Abdel-Hamid, "Thinking in Circles," *American Programmer*, May 1993.

Rembert Aranda, Thomas Fiddaman, and Rogelio Oliva, "Quality Microworlds: modeling the impact of quality initiatives over the software product life cycle," *American Programmer*, May 1993.

Karim J. Chichakly, "The Bifocal Vantage Point: Managing software projects from a systems thinking perspective," *American Programmer*, May 1993.

Kenneth G. Cooper and Thomas W. Mullen, "Swords and Plowshares: the rework cycles of defense and commercial software development projects," *American Programmer*, May 1993.

Ernst W. Diehl, "The Analytical Lens: Strategy-support software to enhance executive dialog and debate," *American Programmer*, May 1993.

Jay Forrester, *Industrial Dynamics* (Cambridge, MA: MIT Press, 1961).

Chi Y. Lin, "Walking on Battlefields: tools for strategic software management," *American Programmer*, May 1993.

G.P. Richardson and G.L. Pugh III, *Introduction to Systems Dynamics Modeling with Dynamo* (Cambridge, MA: MIT Press, 1981).

P.M. Senge, *The Fifth Discipline: The Art and Practice of the Learning Organization* (New York: Doubleday, 1990).

Brad Smith, Nghia Nguyen, and Richard Vidale, "Death of a Software Manager: how to avoid career suicide though dynamic software process modeling," *American Programmer,* May 1993.

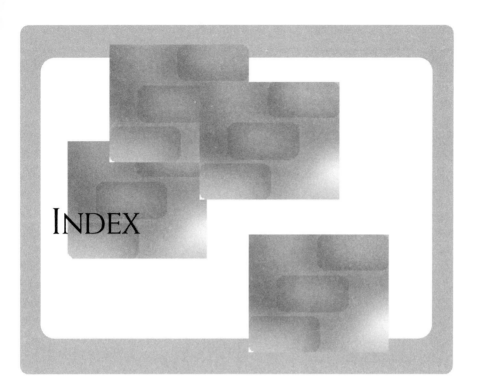

INDEX